FAUNAL STUDIES ON URBAN SITES

THE ANIMAL BONES FROM EXETER

1971 - 1975

MARK MALTBY M.A.

with a contribution by M. WILKINSON
on the Fish Remains

EXETER ARCHAEOLOGICAL REPORTS
VOLUME 2,

Department of Prehistory and Archaeology
University of Sheffield

1979

CONTENTS

LIST OF FIGURES

LIST OF TABLES

vi

FOREWORD

The series of excavations which commenced in 1971 in Exeter in many ways epitomises the problems faced by urban archaeology in the last decade. Up to that time the initiative for archaeological research in the city, if not in Devon, lay with the University of Exeter, in the hands of Lady Aileen Fox, indeed for the two decades after the Second World War Aileen Fox *was* the archaeology of the southwest. When it was realised that major redevelopment was about to take place in central Exeter, it was again Aileen Fox who initiated discussion of financing excavations with the Department of the Environment, and also requested that I, as a newly appointed probationary lecturer in the Department of History, should direct the excavations. In addition the University agreed to give substantial financial aid to the excavations.

At the same time the more adventurous local councils were recognising their obligations to their archaeological heritage, among them Exeter City Council, who, under the initiative of their museum director Mr. Patrick Boylan, appointed a city archaeologist. In the event, Mr. Michael Griffiths did not take up his appointment until the summer of 1971 when excavations had already started. In theory I was to be the over-all director, but in practice two sites needed excavation, and we each took charge of one; myself on the Guildhall Site in Goldsmith Street (GS I, II, III), and he the St. Mary Major Site (MM) near the cathedral, though we were both under joint charge of our respective heads of department, Professor Frank Barlow and Patrick Boylan. On my departure to Sheffield in December 1972 Mike Griffiths took over total charge, including the final phases of GS III. From this time onwards the planning and execution of excavation in the city was in the hands of the City Council, as it should rightly be, for only in this way, within the planning department, can proper provision for archaeological excavation be arranged during redevelopment.

What then of the role of the universities? I hope in part this volume answers some of the questions, as we can provide both the facilities and the staff for the processing of archaeological finds and their publication. But we should not merely be considered as specialists on whom rubbish can be dumped for a 'specialist report' which will be assigned to an appendix and duly ignored, as long as the report is there for appearances sake. Sampling, indeed excavation strategy, can only be undertaken by close on-site cooperation between 'specialist' and excavator, as Mark Maltby's report makes abundantly clear. But there is also a danger that academics will drift out of rescue archaeology through lack of financial support; most funds now go directly to archaeological units, and I for one now use such university funds as I can muster to work abroad where I have more to contribute.

My special interest in the Exeter excavations lay in the socio-economic sphere, of which the animal bones are a major aspect, they were indeed the only group of finds I removed in their totality with me to Sheffield. I may be idealistic in believing that unless an archaeological director is himself capable of basic bone identification, he will be incapable of transmitting enthusiasm to the excavator in the trench, and the bones will end up so mangled as not to be worth the time of study; but I would suggest to many directors, throw them away unless you have some specific questions to ask. The Exeter bones were excavated with care, if sampling techniques are not what we would now demand, and this tradition of care has passed on to the present city archaeologist, Chris Henderson. The recognition of the importance of this bone collection, the most important by far from southwest England, has led the City Museum to accept the responsibility of storing them, though storage problems in Sheffield have caused some damage. As Mark Maltby himself admits, much more can be obtained from them, especially as our theoretical and technical skills develop. On the other hand poorly excavated bones (and pottery) are hardly worth the cardboard boxes that contain them and should be discarded.

The first season in Exeter, based upon the model of Winchester, relied on a large influx of summer volunteers to whom a meagre subsistence was paid. Up to 80 workers were employed at one time, causing problems both of accommodation and control, but by the time GS III was started we were evolving towards the semi-professional small team of workers supplemented by a limited number of volunteers which is now the norm, raising standards of work and efficiency, especially in Exeter where we started with a lack of trained supervisors. But I still view advocates of a fully professional system with suspicion. Such a system, for instance, in Germany has led to a resistance to the introduction of new techniques (e.g. stratigraphy!), and has also divorced archaeology from its social context. A controlled use of local and seasonal volunteers will prevent archaeologists from becoming a brand of bureaucrat, and also allow interaction with local society, which is after all financing the project. Equally I hope the day of 'mass volunteers' are numbered with all the difficulty that implies in communication and control. If the aims and problems are not known, and questioned, by the workers at the trowel face and if volunteers are merely used as uninformed fodder, neither improvement of standards nor social relevance will be achieved.

The late 1960s saw a fundamental realignment of

theoretical aims, and so of methodology in excavation techniques in urban archaeology. The expansion of aims from a narrow historical approach to one embracing a wide range of economic and social questions demanded a shift from the vertical section to the horizontal plan, from trench excavation to open area stripping, and from the start area excavation was employed in Exeter, with all its attendant problems - cost, difficulty of control, lack of rapid 'results' - and only now, in reports such as this on the animal bones, can our concern with late periods such as the seventeenth and eighteenth centuries, or with 'unspectacular' sites such as the Guildhall site at last be really vindicated. The site of visual impact, St. Mary Major, with its substantial remains of Roman masonry, while good for the archaeologists' public image, cannot be understood except in the total context of town houses and slums, cess pits and rubbish dumps. The city can only be viewed as a dynamic whole, both in spatial and chronological terms.

This volume is the second to be produced by the Department of Prehistory and Archaeology in the University of Sheffield, and as General Editor I would like to thank Miranda Barker, Gill Turner, Dorothy Cruse, Anne Hill and Cliff Samson for their help in preparing this volume, and of course to Mark Maltby for long hours of work both on the bones themselves, and on preparing the text for publication. The report has been generously supported by a grant from the Department of the Environment, and our thanks go especially to Sarnia Butcher for supporting what is a venture into an unpredictable area of publication.

Finally, as the publication of my excavations is now in the hands of the Exeter Unit, I would like to take this opportunity to thank my supervisors and assistants who worked for me on the excavation under often difficult and uncomfortable conditions. Eric Wayman, Dave Whipp and Chris Henderson were the main supervisors assisted by Sarah Campbell, Graham Black and John Reading. Stu May, Ann Gentry and Tim Shepherd were in charge of planning, and Sissel Collis assisted by Linda Hollingworth ran the finds shed.

John Collis
November 1979.

PREFACE

It is gratifying to find that many of the reasons I put forward to justify the detailed study of the Exeter animal bones over five years ago are still valid today. I wrote then that the material recently recovered from the excavations presented a rare opportunity to investigate a large and well excavated urban sample which could be used to monitor the exploitation of domestic animals in a major provincial centre throughout a substantial period of its history. It was intended that the analysis would examine possible changes in the meat diet, trends in the size and quality of the stock, various aspects of marketing practices and establish the importance of various species of wild mammals and birds in the diet. At the same time, I stress that the faunal material from Exeter would test the effectiveness of various methods of animal bone analysis when applied to a complex multiperiod site. Undoubtedly the original research proposal in parts reflected the naivety of someone embarking for the first time on a large faunal sample but the dual aims of reconstructing as much information from the Exeter animal bones as possible and, in conjunction with this, examining archaeozoological methodologies remain the major themes of this volume. I still believe that a great deal of information can be extracted from well sampled urban animal bone assemblages to supplement the knowledge about town life sometimes available to us in documentary records. Urban faunal samples, however, present many problems of interpretation and the work in Exeter has demonstrated some of these and has suggested ways of overcoming them I also hope others will benefit from my mistakes! As well as sheding some light on several aspects of Exeter's and Devon's agricultural history, I regard this work as a case study which I hope will be of value for current and future archaeozoological research on urban (and indeed rural) samples.

It is perhaps necessary to explain briefly how this volume came to take on its shape. The analysis of the Exeter animal bones began in October 1974 and formed the basis of a M.A. thesis in the Department of Prehistory and Archaeology at Sheffield University. The data presented in this volume rely heavily on that research (Maltby 1977), although some minor changes in phasing have since been taken into account. The layout of the book also remains substantially unaltered from that of the thesis, although Chapters 2-7 have all been revised and updated to a greater or lesser degree. Mike Wilkinson has now investigated the fish bones from these excavations and his report has been incorporated in Chapter 7. The introduction (Chapter 1) and the conclusion (Chapter 8) have been completely rewritten and extended to cover several more general issues raised by this research. I make no apology for the large number of tables that appear at the end of this volume. The bones were not computer recoreded and these tables, besides being essential aids to the discussion in the text, should also be regarded as the archive for this material and thus easily accessible to archaeozoologists working on subsequent material from Exeter and also as comparative data for others interested in animal bone analysis in Britain and elsewhere. This is the first monograph published in this country concerned solely with British archaeozoological data. It is to be hoped that it will not be the last. At the same time, I hope that this work will not be regarded simply as a glorified specialist's report - a superbreed of the cursory appendix to the main site report, to which many faunal studies are still doomed If nothing else, I believe the work in Exeter has shown the potential such studies have in understanding many important aspects of complex societies.

The analysis was funded initially by a Department of Education and Science research studentship grant and then by a grant from the Department of the Environment. I also received generous financial assistance from my parents. I am grateful to Mike Griffiths, Chris Henderson, John Allan and Paul Bidwell for allowing me to study material from sites and for providing dating and other information about the bones. The chapter on bird and fish remains would not have been possible but for the detailed work on Mike Wilkinson on the fish bones and the kindness and patience of Don Bramwell, who guided me during my first faltering steps of bird bone identification and allowed me access to his comparative collection - my thanks to both. Robin Dennell kindly made available unpublished data from Plymouth. My thanks to Jennie Coy and Clive Gamble for their comments on earlier drafts of some of the Chapters. May I second the general editor's thanks to Miranda Barker, Dorothy Cruse, Gill Turner, Anne Hill and Cliff Samson for their work on the preparation of this volume for publication. Finally, special thanks to Graeme Barker, for his advice, encouragement and comments during the research and to John Collis, whose foresight in realising the value of the Exeter animal bones initiated this reasearch and who, as general editor, has guided this work through to final publication.

J.M.M.
December 1979.

1.

INTRODUCTION

The study of animal bones from archaeological sites is, to use a common economic cliche, very much a growth industry. During the last twenty years such studies have gradually become recognised as an essential aid towards the understanding of prehistoric and early historic populations. Much of the pioneering work was done in Germany and is epitomised by the production of detailed reports such as that for the iron age oppidum at Manching (Boessneck *et al.* 1971). In Britain, the value of economic and environmental data from archaeological sites was not realised until somewhat later. Previously, only a handful of such studies had been carried out and many of those consisted of short and cursory appendices to site reports. After years of such neglect the examination of animal bones has become much more common during the last decade. Ideally, the recovery of faunal remains should play an important part of the excavation of any site where they are preserved and an archaeozoologist should be consulted at the planning stage and during the course of an excavation to discuss recovery and sampling strategies. But, despite a growing acceptance by archaeologists that faunal studies are worthwhile, there are still those who remain sceptical about their value.

In addition, it is not surprising that faunal material from prehistoric sites has received much more attention than that from sites dated to Roman and more recent times. This situation has arisen because of the assumption that sufficient information about diet, livestock husbandry and other related topics can be found in documentary sources and that the collection and examination of animal bones are therefore of little consequence in these periods. This is a mistaken assumption. Such detailed documentary evidence is relatively rare and, where it does exist, it does not often relate directly to the specific questions being asked about an archaeological sample, which offer an insight into certain aspects of life that documentary sources are unlikely to provide. It is also interesting to compare the two types of evidence where they overlap and they should be used to complement each other where possible.

The scepticism of some archaeologists is perhaps to be expected when one considers the course of British archaeology during the last ten years. The growth of interest in faunal studies has coincided with the development of intensive rescue archaeology in both urban and rural settings. The recovery and examination of animal bones are expensive and time-consuming tasks for archaeologists with a limited budget and a minimal amount of time for excavation and they have the right to expect that their investments in this respect should provide dividends. Yet, although a number of site reports has been published on some relatively small samples and some specialised papers on particular aspects of faunal studies have appeared, very few major site studies

have been produced in the last decade. Large faunal samples are essential, if we are to answer satisfactorily the detailed questions such analyses raise, or test sophisticated models concerning animal husbandry and marketing practices. However, extensive reports on animal bone assemblages of over 20,000 fragments have been limited to those from Portchester Castle (Grant 1975, 1976) and Melbourne Street, Southampton (Bourdillon and Coy *in press*). The situation will improve during the next few years as reports from extensive urban excavations at Winchester, London and elsewhere are published together with those from several important iron age, Roman and Saxon sites. At present, however, rescue archaeologists are faced with the problem of retrieving good faunal samples without a full appreciation of what they can achieve.

Bearing this in mind, the 75,000 animal bone fragments recovered from the excavations of the Exeter Archaeological Field Unit between 1971 and 1975 are important for two main reasons. In the first place, their study affords the opportunity to review the methodologies employed by archaeozoologists with particular regard to urban excavations. Secondly, they provide information about a fundamental aspect of life in the Roman and medieval periods. Exeter, the county town of Devon in southwest England, was first a Roman legionary base and then a *civitas* — a major provincial centre. Medieval Exeter was a thriving market town, which ranked as one of the largest in England. Later, it became the focus for an important cloth trade. In all, the faunal sample spanned a period of 1,800 years and provides an insight into the diet of the urban population and the agricultural economy of the surrounding area throughout that time.

What questions should be asked of the faunal samples from urban sites? Many of them relate to the everyday lives of their inhabitants. What was their diet? Did they supplement their meat supplies with the successes of hunting and fowling expeditions? Did a person's prosperity or status in society influence his diet? How were the domestic stock slaughtered, butchered and marketed? Were cattle most important for beef, their hides, dairy products or as working animals? Were sheep bred principally for meat or wool or milk or cheese? Identification of the fragments of animal bone can establish the relative importance of the different species. Recurring cut marks on bones provide information about butchery practices. Examination of the teeth and the epiphyseal fusion of the limb bones can reveal the age of the animals at death. Consequently, it is theoretically possible to reconstruct the mortality rates of the stock and understand their economic implications. Metrical analysis of bones and teeth can provide information about the size and quality of

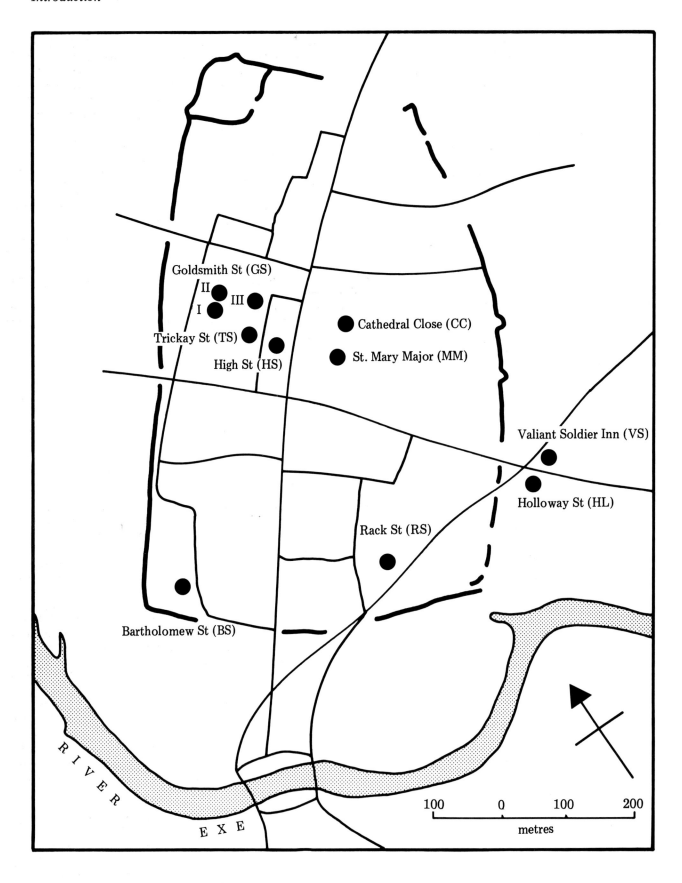

Figure 1   Map of sites under investigation at Exeter.

the stock, the ratios of female and male animals and even the different types of animal in existence at the time.

These are all important questions which faunal analysis should attempt to answer. Yet, as with other archaeological finds, the remains represent only a fragmentary proportion of the original data. The archaeologist is faced with the problem of interpreting postholes as meaningful structures and explaining their function. The expert in ceramics is expected to produce insights into the typology, provenance, dating, function and other aspects of pottery from the study of accumulations of very fragmentary sherds. Similarly, the archaeozoologist has to reconstruct all the aspects of faunal interpretation from inherently imperfect data. The rapid growth of intensive faunal studies has resulted in a number of methodologies to deal with the various aspects involved. Because the discipline is relatively new, there has been little attempt at standardisation. The approach has been one of trial and error and this trend will probably continue for some time. For there is no established way to investigate animal bones. Several detailed reviews of the methods and problems of faunal studies have been produced in the last few years (Chaplin 1971; Payne 1972b; Uerpmann 1973). These are all useful general surveys of archaeozoology but the study of urban assemblages produces additional dimensions that also have to be considered. It seems appropriate, therefore, to use the Exeter material as a case study and discuss at some length the methods of analysis employed. This gives the opportunity to review with the benefit of hindsight the methods originally used in the research, it is to be hoped in an objective way. Some of the methods are not now recommended for other urban sites, some could be modified or adapted in different ways, others are considered essential in the study of complex assemblages.

THE PROBLEMS OF QUANTITATIVE ANALYSIS

Quantification of animal bones involves their identification and recording and then the analysis of the material to assess the relative importance of each species on a site. It should also involve intra- and inter-site studies to assess how much variation there is in the animal bone assemblages.

The context of the sample

The archaeology of a town presents enormous sampling problems. Industrial areas, market places, public and ceremonial buildings, town defences and residential suburbs are just a few of the locations that may be excavated. These can be expected to produce a wide variety of material. The same applies to the faunal material found associated with them. The animal bones deposited from the slaughterhouse, the market, the butcher and the kitchens of rich or poor households may be completely different from each other. Accordingly the bone assemblage from one area of the town may not be typical of the rest and it is dangerous to read too much into such results. Conversely the existence of lateral variation is of interest and should be investigated thoroughly.

Exeter provided the opportunity to compare the faunal remains from the following nine sites:

1. Goldsmith St. Areas I-III (abbreviation: GS I-III)
2. Trickhay St. (TS)
3. High St. (HS)
4. St. Mary Major (MM)   ) Cathedral
5. Cathedral Close/Cathedral Yard (CC/CY)) Close
6. Rack St. (RS)
7. Holloway St. (HL)
8. Bartholomew St. (BS)
9. The Valiant Soldier site, Holloway St. (VS)

All these sites were excavated between 1971-1975 by Exeter University and the Exeter Archaeological Field Unit. They are situated in different parts of the city (Figure 1) and produced a wide variety of structures, pits and other features. The medieval and postmedieval bone samples investigated were collected mainly from the neighbouring GS and TS sites, both of which produced an abundance of material. The medieval deposits of the smaller HS site and the seventeenth century levels of the VS site were also studied in this analysis. The Roman sample consisted of material obtained from all areas except the VS site.

The excavated Roman deposits varied a good deal in their nature. The MM site produced the spectacular discovery of part of the Military Baths, which were converted into a Basilica and Forum in approximately 75 A. D. The GS and TS sites were residential areas until the fourth century when a cattleyard and associated gullies and ditches were constructed on the sites. The RS material was obtained mostly from the large defensive ditch, which incorporated part of the legionary defences and which was infilled from about 75 A.D. onwards. The remaining sites were predominantly residential areas.

The vast majority of the medieval and postmedieval material came from pits filled with cess or other domestic waste. Hardly any structural features survive because of postmedieval terracing. In the sixteenth century pottery kilns were constructed on the GS III site, while there is evidence that much of the GS I-II site was used for horticultural purposes. There is documentary evidence for stables on the TS site in the postmedieval period (Collis 1972; Henderson *pers. comm.*).

Investigation of the medieval pottery has not given any indication of major differences in social status before the sixteenth century on any of the sites investigated; imported vessels and fine jugs occurred in similar quantities in all areas. In the fourteenth century the TS site did possess large stone-lined pits, which did not occur on the GS III site until the sixteenth century. It is possible that the former area was more affluent than the latter in late medieval times. In the sixteenth century the GS III site produced many rich finds including Rhenish imports and the late seventeenth century levels of the TS site yielded objects of Chinese porcelain and glass. These wealthy finds were dated to a period of great prosperity in Exeter when there was a boom in the cloth trading industry in Devon. In contrast the pottery and other finds from the late seventeenth and eighteenth century contexts on the GS I-II site were conspicuously of a lesser quality. This appears to correlate with documentary evidence which describes the parish in which this site lies as being poorer and possibly subject to overcrowding at the time (Allan *pers. comm.*).

Preservation

The majority of animal bone originally deposited on any archaeological site does not survive. This stark reality has to be accepted by archaeozoologists. A whole series of physical, chemical and human agencies combine to destroy all but a fraction of the original number of bone fragments. The causes of destruction have been discussed in detail (Binford and Bertram 1977) and need not be elaborated here. Suffice it to say that the major agents of attrition are poor soil conditions, the erosion and weathering of unburied or shallowly buried bone, gnawing by carnivores and rodents, burning and fragmentation. Unfortunately these processes attack bone elements differentially. Some bones have a better chance of survival than others. Those most at risk are the small or more porous and less dense fragments. Bird, small mammal and fish bones are particularly vulnerable, as are the unfused limb bones of young animals of all species. In general, any fragment containing a high proportion of spongy cancellous bone (such as epiphyses, ribs and vertebrae) has a poorer chance of survival than those which consist mainly of cortical bone. All faunal samples are therefore biased towards the denser bones. The extent of this bias depends on the degree of attrition. Accurate methods of measuring these taphonomic processes have not yet been devised and research into the problem is only at an early stage. Until this has advanced, absolute reconstruction of the bone originally deposited is impossible using the methodology commonly practised on faunal data. Nonetheless, it is possible to observe the standard of preservation of the bone fragments and compare the evidence from different sites and periods in relative terms. Urban sites often offer a better chance of bone survival than others, since a lot of rubbish was buried deeply in pits and wells and other features where preservation conditions are good. Bone is soon destroyed if left lying open to the elements. The problem of extensive urban archaeology, however, is that the preservation conditions may vary significantly between widely separated areas and cause difficulties in inter-site comparisons.

The preservation of bone on all sites in Exeter was extremely good in general. Observed erosion on the bones investigated was confined to relatively few features, usually in association with slowly accumulated layers, in which the bones had probably lain on or near the ground surface for some time. The material of postmedieval date was generally in a better state of preservation than most of the Roman material; but the improvement was slight and usually only affected the results to a small degree. A few bones had evidence of gnawing on them, mostly by dogs. Most of the bone was unaffected by this, however, and this suggests that a lot of the material was buried soon after disposal. Dogs and rodents will have completely destroyed other fragments, however. There were a few cases of burnt charred bone in the deposits, the most numerous examples coming from the extremely rich GS III F.228 and TS F.316 pits, in which certain layers also produced many bones that had concretions adhering to them. These exceptions apart, the large majority of the bone was in a good but fragmentary state of preservation.

Recovery methods

The recovery methods can affect the nature of the faunal material studied. Payne (1972a, 1975) has shown that unsieved faunal samples tend to be biased towards the larger mammals because the bones of smaller mammals, birds and fish are more likely to be overlooked during excavation. The extent of such a bias also varies according to how well the bone is preserved. Sieving experiments at the early medieval settlement at Dorestad, in the Netherlands, revealed that the unsieved material was biased in favour of cattle and horse in comparison with pig, sheep and goat. Water-sieving produced an enormous amount of fish, bird and small mammal bones, of which very few were recovered from the initial excavation (Clason and Prummel 1977). Urban rescue archaeologists can rarely afford the time and labour to water-sieve all deposits. Such material also takes much longer to process and study and there is a limit to the amount of information that can be gained from its study. As Payne (1975: 16-17) points out, the answer must lie in sample-sieving and a flexible approach to such a strategy is needed.

Although the majority of the deposits in Exeter were not sieved, some sections of RS F.363 were both dry- and wet-sieved. The results obtained from these samples differed little from the unsieved material. However, this feature - a large defensive ditch that was deliberately infilled from about 75 A. D. onwards - is exceptional in that it was used as a depository for a vast amount of cattle mandible, skull and metapodia fragments and very little ordinary kitchen refuse was found in it. A limited amount of wet-sieving was carried out on GS I and GS II, but the return was so minimal that it was abandoned. Consequently, the sieving experiments must remain inconclusive with regard to the sample as a whole. It is fair to say that the standard of recovery and preservation at Exeter was very good; nevertheless it has to be assumed that a lesser proportion of the bones belonging to smaller animals, birds and fish was recovered, although the amount of bias is uncertain. Sample-sieving of some of the richest waterlogged pits probably would have increased the representation of the smallest animals and have provided additional information about the fauna in the deposits. However, assuming that the standard of excavation was similar in deposits of all periods, it is possible to make direct comparisons of the samples collected from them and to observe the relative changes in the assemblages. Detailed analysis of the Exeter deposits was able to test this assumption and in general found it to be true. Variations in the faunal assemblage in most cases could be explained by differential preservation and disposal practices rather than recovery bias.

The dating of the sample

The complexity of urban sites provides great problems of phasing and dating. It is very difficult to relate the phased stratigraphy of one site to another and the archaeozoologist has to rely heavily upon the dating evidence provided by the pottery and other artifacts. Often the dating of such objects is open to question and this causes further difficulties. Of even greater concern are the factors of redeposition and contamination of layers with material of other dates. To counter this, special care is needed to observe the fills of the deposits and the preservation of the bone, which can often indicate the likelihood of contamination.

The Exeter sample was divided into three major periods, Roman (about 55 A.D. to early fifth century), medieval (eleventh to fifteenth centuries) and postmedieval (sixteenth to late eighteenth centuries). Where possible these periods were divided into phases which spanned 50 years. This was not practicable in all cases since the pottery evidence, upon which the dating principally relied, was not always diagnostic to a particular 50 year period. When this occurred certain phases were extended to cover a longer time span. Details of these divisions will be given in the following chapter.

All deposits that were not securely dated were not considered in the analysis. Some of the Roman features examined may have had a little later medieval material in their make-up but the percentage of this would have been too small to bias the results significantly. Many of the early medieval features contained residual Roman pottery; indeed sometimes over 50% of the sherds were Roman in origin. However, many of the pits involved, especially those dated to the eleventh and early twelfth centuries, had black anaerobic fills which included much bone but very little pottery. The Roman residual sherds therefore tended to form a high percentage of the total potsherds but it is thought that the percentage of Roman bone in those early medieval features was of a much lower order, probably negligible in many cases. Prior to the twelfth century there was so little contemporary pottery in circulation that the presence of a few Roman sherds tended to overemphasise the amount of residual material present (Allan *pers. comm.*). Certainly, the amount of residual bone cannot be estimated on the percentage of pottery alone. In addition, the fills of these pits contrasted markedly with other features which did contain redeposited Roman material and which were not considered in the analysis. The medieval features which contained relatively high proportions of Roman pottery showed no significant variation from those with no residual material whatsoever, as far as the faunal remains were concerned. On the other hand, these medieval samples generally showed consistent variations from the Roman faunal material, thus supporting their independent and later origins.

THE METHODS OF QUANTITATIVE ANALYSIS

Any analysis of 75,000 items of data requires careful consideration of methodology. This has to be designed to take into account the complexity of the variations involved. Most of the published bone reports quantify the material by counting the number of fragments and recording the percentages of each species identified. Alternatively, various methods of estimating the minimum number of individuals of each species are employed. The percentage figures are then used to draw conclusions about the relative or absolute abundance of each species and their importance to the diet and economy. In the case of a multi-period site, the figures from each period are compared with each other. Such simplistic comparisons, however, are meaningless unless it can be shown that the samples are unaffected by variations in fragmentation, preservation, recovery methods, butchery practices and other possible biases. To do this the faunal analyst has to examine in more detail the type of bone fragments recovered. Many reports list the number of fragments of each bone element but such statistics are rarely analysed in any depth. It is only by such a study, however, that any real understanding of the sample can be obtained. This analysis formed a substantial part of the research on the animal bones from Exeter and the methods used warrant some discussion.

Identification

The identification of animal bones depends on an adequate comparative skeleton collection. Some fragments are more identifiable than others and often a time factor is involved in how long an archaeozoologist spends in attempting to identify each fragment to a particular species. Such considerations on the Exeter material meant that ribs and vertebrae (other than the atlas, axis and sacrum) were counted but not assigned to species. It is difficult in many cases to differentiate between certain species from the fragmentary remains of ribs in particular. The numbers of rib and vertebrae fragments are included in the number of unidentified fragments in the appropriate tables, of which they constituted between 60 to 90%. The decision to include vertebrae among the unidentified material was one enforced by pressures of time and by some inadequacies in the comparative reference collection originally used. This policy is not recommended for other sites, however, since vertebrae are good meat bones and provide important information about carcass disposal and butchery techniques and should therefore be identified to species where possible. The remainder of the unidentified material consisted mostly of small splinters of bone, which could not be assigned to species but which, like the ribs and vertebrae, could often be categorised as 'large mammal' (cattle, red deer, horse), 'medium mammal' (sheep, goat, fallow deer, roe deer, pig, dog), 'small mammal' (hare, cat, rabbit, rodent, etc.) and 'unidentified bird'.

Determination between sheep and goat is very difficult from bone evidence since differences between certain bones of the two species are very small and the fragmentary nature of an archaeological sample means that many specimens cannot be assigned with any confidence to one of the two species. Their bones will henceforth be referred to as 'sheep/goat'.

Analysis by fragment count

Each bone fragment examined was recorded and wherever possible assigned to species. Quantification by employing a simple count of fragments is still the most common method of analysis but it has recognised drawbacks. Estimating the percentage of each species from the number of identified fragments has been criticised because, since any bone can break up into several fragments, a large number of fragments may represent just one animal. A few animals may thus be represented by a disproportionately high number of identified fragments. The degree of variation may also vary between species. The following hypothetical example is given by Chaplin (1971:65-66): 'It may therefore be expected that if a usable joint is about the size of a leg of lamb, the femur, in the case of the sheep, will probably survive butchery and cooking, whereas that of the ox may be cut into a dozen or more pieces. In many cases the leg of beef may be boned out before the meat joints are cut and the bone chopped up to provide a meal in itself. Of these dozen pieces, perhaps five (to be conservative) will be identifiable compared to only one intact bone of the sheep. There is therefore a bias if the species ratio is based upon the number of fragments'.

Of course in actual practice the situation is not as clear cut as this. There is usually a good deal of variation in the size of fragments from any particular bone. Nevertheless it is true to say that the fragments method of counting does favour the largest mammals, in particular cattle, rather than pig and sheep/goat. This has to be borne in mind when considering the results.

Other problems concerning this method are easier to overcome. Certain species possess more bones in their skeletons than others. For example, a horse has twelve phalanges, cattle and other ungulates 24, a pig has 48 and a dog 52-58 (Payne 1972b:68). Smaller discrepancies occur also in the number of metapodials and teeth which each species possesses. Pigs, dogs and cats also have a fibula, whereas cattle, sheep/goat and deer only possess the vestigial remains of this bone which are very rarely recovered. Generally the bones involved did not occur in sufficient numbers to bias the sample significantly. Reference will be made to any feature or group of features that were exceptions to the rule.

A similar methodological problem relates to the occurrence of the burials of animals amongst other faunal remains. Several burials of animals were found in the deposits. For instance, from the Roman period there were three immature pig skeletons of late first century date (73 fragments), 42 fragments from one badger skeleton and 24 from two dogs, the badger and dogs being of third century date. From the fourth century levels another burial of a dog provided ten fragments and a partially preserved woodmouse skeleton contributed twenty. The pattern was similar in the medieval period, in which a dog burial of late thirteenth century date contributed thirteen fragments to the total. Two cat burials, the first of twelfth century date and the second of late twelfth-early thirteenth century date, contributed 35 and 21 fragments respectively. None of these animals bore evidence of butchery marks and it is clear that they were not part of the food supply, having in most cases been simply dumped on the rubbish heap. Obviously the presence of such skeletons inflates the total number of fragments of the species in question to a higher level than is truly representative and accordingly biases the results. The number of fragments from these burials was recorded but should be discounted from any overall assessment of the number of fragments. The presence of a burial or burials in a particular phase will be indicated in the relevant table by an asterisk against the species. Fortunately the five immature pig burials (three of Roman, one of medieval and one of postmedieval date) were the only examples of burials of the major stock animals, so the overall assessment of these was virtually unaffected. Most of the skeletons belonged to cats, dogs and other animals that are not considered to have been butchered for food. It is probable that many of the other bones of these species recovered from the excavations also belonged to burials but not enough of the skeleton has survived to establish this fact. This situation reached its greatest complexity in some of the large postmedieval deposits. For example, there was a big concentration of dog remains in TS F.316 (late seventeenth century), 265 fragments from a minimum number of 24 individuals were recovered. There seems no doubt that a large number of dogs was dumped in the pit but it is difficult to establish exactly how many since the skeletons were so mixed. The presence of such concentrations of burials undoubtedly biased the sample as a whole, especially when employing the fragments method of counting.

Analysis of the minimum number of individuals

Discussions of the methodology, interpretation and justification of this second method of quantification have appeared regularly during the last few years (Chaplin 1971; Payne 1972b; Grayson 1973; Uerpmann 1973; Casteel 1977). The aim of such calculations is self-explanatory and has the advantage of eliminating many of the problems of fragmentation from the analysis. It has to be emphasised that the method is merely a device to quantify the data in a formalised manner and the results should not be treated literally. The statement that a minimum number of 60 cattle and 30 pigs was represented on a site does not mean that cattle were twice as numerous as pigs. It merely states that the method of calculation used in the analysis produced these results. Given similar preservation, recovery practices, methodology and other factors, the results can be compared with those of another period or site. As with the simple count of fragments, it is the establishment of the homogeneity of the different samples that is the major problem.

The minimum number of individuals can be calculated in a variety of ways. Applied to the same material they may produce different results. Each method is subject to the vagaries of sample size and aggregation of the sampling units (Casteel 1977). Archaeozoologists should state clearly the particular methods they employ. The method adopted on the Exeter material was as follows.

The minimum number for each bone element (mandible, humerus, etc.) was established for each species for every individual feature. This was achieved by separating left-sided fragments from right, counting shaft fragments as well as those with articular surfaces still present. Fusion data and, in the case of jaws and teeth, evidence of tooth eruption were also taken into consideration.

The minimum number of animals belonging to a particular phase on a site was calculated for each bone type by adding together the numbers attained for each feature. This cumulative process assumed that there was no admixing of the same bone elements in different deposits of the same date. This is undoubtedly a false assumption. It can be argued justifiably that, for example, five fragments of the same cattle tibia may have been scattered in five different features and that theoretically the cumulative method of analysis may suggest that they came from five individuals. However, on a complex urban site often dealing with phases of 50 years or more, the sample of animal bones recovered is such a small proportion of the bones originally brought to the town that it is extremely unlikely that this factor would bias the results significantly. It should also be observed that had time allowed large numbers of measurements to be taken for each bone element, the minimum number of individuals would have been substantially increased in many features, since the discrepancy in size would not have permitted as many bones to be 'paired' with fragments from the opposite side of the body.

The percentages obtained for the various species for each phase by this method were taken from the most common bone element represented. The type of bone varied between species and between different phases and sites. Details of these for cattle, sheep/goat and pig will be found in Tables 7, 8, 9 and 10. In phases where material from more than one site was examined, the minimum number of individuals represented on each site was added together, irrespective of the bone element which produced this figure. This assumed that parts of the same animal were not scattered throughout the various sites. This again is probably a false assumption but the chances of this seriously biasing the results are small.

As is to be expected, there was a marked difference between the percentages obtained by a count of fragments and those calculated from the minimum number of individuals. The levels of cattle were much lower according to the latter method, with a fall of over 25% in some cases below the figure reached from the count of fragments. This discrepancy between the two methods has also been noted by Higham (1967: 85-86). It can be explained to a large extent by the fact that bovine bones, being relatively larger, have a greater chance of breaking into fragments that cannot be paired when calculating the minimum numbers. It was observed, for example, that whereas in certain features three fragments of sheep/goat or pig tibia belonging to the same side of the body would produce a minimum number of two or three individuals, three fragments of cattle tibia more often could only be given a minimum number of one, since they could have belonged to different parts of the same bone. This applied to all long bone, jaw and skull fragments. For every 100 fragments of a species identified, an average minimum number of 6.72 individuals was established for sheep/goat, 7.82 for pig but only 4.54 for cattle. A drawback in using this method of calculating the minimum numbers is that variability in context size may affect the results. The ratio of minimum numbers to fragments is higher in smaller features than in larger ones. Consequently, if the size of the bone assemblages in individual features varies significantly on different sites or in different periods, the results of the minimum number calculations may be influenced. More detailed studies of this ratio on the Exeter material did show a fairly consistent pattern between the different phases and sites and most of the variability could be explained by small sample size in some of the phases rather than by any dramatic changes in the fragmentation of the material.

One of the acknowledged problems of the minimum numbers method of analysis is that it overestimates the importance of the rarer species in the sample. Reference to Tables 1-6, 11, 14, 17, 20, 23, 26, 29, 30, 33, etc. will demonstrate this. Percentage figures obtained from small samples are thus unreliable. Bird bones present problems for the same reason. Because of the large number of species involved, the minimum numbers method tends to overstate their importance. Consequently it was decided to treat their remains separately.

The various minimum numbers methods of quantification have been claimed to be more reliable than a simple count of fragments and they do take into account more of the variables encountered in faunal assemblages. This advantage is, however, negated to a certain extent by the fact that, by reducing the figures for estimating the relative importance of each species by about 90% when compared to the fragment method of counting, only the larger samples carry any statistical importance.

Statistical tests

The two types of analysis described above were used as the basic quantitative methods for the faunal data from Exeter. However, to test their suitability to deal with complex urban samples, certain statistical techniques have to be applied. Two main considerations governed the type of test that was used. The first was that ideally the tests should be relatively straightforward to give a quick indication of inter-site variability and at the same time give a rough guide to the causes of this variability. Chi-square tests were found to be a useful means towards this aim. The second consideration was the size of the samples, which limited the range of tests that could be used, particularly with regard to the minimum numbers method. The statistical analysis was therefore restricted to the major stock animals — cattle, sheep/goat and pig. The samples of all the other identified species were too small to make similar analysis worthwhile.

In such tests, ideally each bone element should be considered separately. However, unless the samples are very large, the number involved would be too small for statistical tests on some of the less common elements to carry much weight. Consequently, the bone elements had to be amalgamated into categories and the following subdivisions of the skeletons were selected for study and comparison:

Category 1 — the mandible, loose teeth, maxilla and other skull fragments.
Category 2 — the scapula, humerus, pelvis and femur.
Category 3 — the radius, ulna and tibia.
Category 4 — the metapodials.
Category 5 — the carpals and tarsals.
Category 6 — the phalanges and sesamoids.
Category 7 — other bones (atlas, axis, sacrum, patella, fibula).

These categories were chosen in order to group together bones of similar uses and functions. Thus the parts of the carcass from which most meat can be obtained are included in Category 2 (although depending on butchery methods, both the scapula and pelvis can be treated as waste material). Category 3 consists of meat bones of a lesser quality. The other categories generally have little meat value, although both the skulls and feet can be boiled up for brawn and similar products. The phalanges were placed in a separate category from the metapodials since they may have served a different purpose. Cattle phalanges, for example, are often boiled up for glue, whereas the metapodia, especially of sheep/goat and cattle, offer good raw material for bone tool and ornament manufacture. These categories were used as

the basis for testing both methods of quantitative analysis. They were designed to recognise the occurrence of lateral variation and suggest the principal causes. Subsequent multivariate analysis on faunal material from Exeter and other sites has suggested that these subdivisions are probably too crude (Maltby *in preparation*) and the bone categories should be divided still further. Some of the results of such tests are discussed in Chapter 2.

Ideally too, the bone assemblages of each feature should be considered separately. Once again, however, the logistics of sample size prevented this. Instead, for each phase the samples were subdivided by site and compared. Obviously, variations can occur at intra-site level as well and should be taken into consideration. Such phenomena were noted and will be discussed at the appropriate point.

The number of fragments for each of the seven categories was totalled in each of the principal stock species. To test for lateral variation within each phase or longer period, the proportions of the categories for each site were compared with the grand total for that phase or period. Chi-square calculations were employed to test whether the observed variations were significant. Exactly the same procedure was carried out on the minimum numbers method. The minimum numbers obtained for each bone element within each category were added together to obtain the sum of the minimum numbers (S. M.). The category proportions of these in each phase were then compared using chi-square calculations for each species in turn. The analysis was therefore designed to test the null hypothesis that, for each species, the proportions of the seven categories were similar on each site in the particular phase or period under consideration. In cases where the statistical tests confirmed this hypothesis, one was entitled to accept that the deposits contained a homogeneous sample of bones.

The results of these tests will be discussed in detail later but they revealed that there was often a significant degree of variation between features and sites dated to the same phase. This lateral variation is to be expected in a complex urban site. It emphasises the limitations of sampling only a restricted area on any large site, since the excavated area may not be representative of the whole settlement. It also calls for a cautious approach where two different sites are to be compared. In order for the comparison to have any validity, not only do the preservation conditions, excavation techniques and methods of analysis need to be similar, but the two samples should also show similarity in the proportions of the different bones represented in each of the major species. A simple comparison of the number of fragments or the minimum number of individuals is not in itself sufficient: in the Exeter sample it was found that even in phases where there was close agreement in the percentage of the animals represented on the different sites, it did not necessarily mean that the samples were similar in content.

The same considerations have to be taken into account when comparing material from different periods. Percentages obtained from simple counts of fragments or by analyses of minimum numbers of individuals cannot be compared directly, if the samples from which they are obtained differ significantly in their constituent parts.

The tests devised for the detection of variation in the samples were experimental. More sophisticated statistical methods can be developed to study these, provided the samples are of sufficient magnitude. The categories, for example, can be further subdivided in such analyses and correlations between the relative frequencies of individual bone elements can be compared. The tests were sufficient, however, to demonstrate the variations in the Exeter faunal assemblage and give some indication of the causes. They certainly demonstrated that, if large multi-period faunal samples are to be subject to quantitative analysis, or if assemblages from different sites are to be compared, the usual methods of such analyses have to be extended to deal with them in a meaningful manner.

THE STUDY OF THE INDIVIDUAL SPECIES

The problems and methods of the study of the individual species will be discussed in more detail in Chapters 3 to 7. This section will therefore be confined to a brief outline of the particular methods employed on the Exeter material.

Ageing methods

There are two ways of ageing animals from bone fragments currently employed by archaeozoologists: the first is to study tooth eruption and tooth wear, the second is to examine the evidence of epiphyseal fusion of the long bones. Both methods were employed on this sample.

Six stages of tooth eruption were selected for cattle and pig. Both mandibles and maxillae were examined in order to discover which of the stages had been reached. It was then possible to estimate the percentage of animals killed before each of the six stages had been attained. Jaws were often incomplete and this factor sometimes made it impossible to determine whether or not certain of the eruption stages had been reached. For instance many cattle jaws just had one or more of their permanent molars (M1-M3) intact and in wear. These jaws produced no direct evidence as to whether the fourth premolar (P4), which has a later development than the permanent molars in cattle, was also in wear or not. Consequently in the tables, where applicable, a minimum and maximum percentage of animals killed at each stage of tooth eruption is given.

It is apparent that when a large number of jaws gives insufficient evidence, any conclusions made on the ageing data will in consequence be rather vague. Accordingly, the wear patterns on selected samples of cattle and pig mandibles were studied using the method devised by Grant on the Portchester Castle bone sample (Grant 1975: 437-450). Using this method it was possible to estimate much more closely how many of the jaws would have reached the various stages and also, especially in the case of cattle, how long an animal lived after its tooth eruption sequence was complete.

Absolute ageing of domestic animals from archaeological sites is notoriously difficult. Variations in nutrition, breed and stock management all influence the rate of tooth eruption. To use modern figures from improved stock as absolute figures is known to be misleading. The use of nineteenth century data may be of more value (Silver 1969: 295-296) but it is nevertheless impossible to be certain of the true age of tooth eruption during any of the periods. This should be remembered when reference is made to the ages of cattle and pig in the later chapters.

Similar stages of tooth eruption and wear were established for the sheep/goat jaws. More detailed analyses have been attempted in recent years on these. For example, Ewbank *et al.* (1964) devised a detailed method, which divided the tooth eruption sequence into 26 stages with estimated ages for each stage. Carter (1975) adapted and modified this sequence and also measured the heights of the P4, M1, M2, M3 and p4 (fourth deciduous premolar) from the highest point of the crown to the division of the roots. By assuming that the wear on these teeth produced a fairly uniform decline in

height, the method theoretically can calculate the age of a mandible or maxilla. Adopting a rather slower rate of tooth eruption than that allowed for by Ewbank *et al.*, Carter has claimed that a jaw with all three permanent molars intact can be aged to within a month with 80% confidence when applied to sheep jaws of iron age to medieval date in the Thames Valley region. This experimental method was tested on the material from Exeter with some interesting results.

Two other methods of studying sheep mandibles were taken into account. Both of these (Grant 1975; Payne 1973) rely on the study of the tooth eruption sequence and the wear patterns of the cheek teeth. It was possible to compare the results of Grant's and Carter's methods on some of the medieval material.

None of the methods established with any certainty the true age of the animals brought to the town. Research into the absolute ageing of teeth from archaeological sites is needed urgently. The various methods were able, however, to record the relative changes in mortality patterns and these were used to infer changes in the exploitation and marketing of the stock.

Epiphyseal fusion occurs on all mammalian long bones. A similar process occurs in bird bones as well. In mammals some epiphyses, for example the distal humerus and proximal radius, fuse at a much earlier age than others, such as the two epiphyses of the femur. It is possible, by grouping together epiphyses of approximately the same fusion age, to estimate the percentage of animals slaughtered before a particular fusion stage took place. Once again the ages given to these stages are adapted from data obtained from modern 'scrub' crossbred animals, which through improved breeding and better nutrition may have faster rates of development than animals of Roman and medieval date (Silver 1969: 285-288). Nevertheless, they can provide a general indication of the culling pattern. The percentages obtained for both ageing methods should be considered as the minimum figures, since in an unsieved sample the smaller and more fragile bones and jaws of the younger animals have less chance of recovery.

The study of epiphyseal fusion data is, however, less reliable than that of tooth eruption. Differential preservation of the long bones has a significant bearing on the results. Epiphyses with later fusion ages are more vulnerable to destruction than those which fuse at a comparatively early age. This causes discrepancies in the results, which will be discussed in the appropriate sections.

Metrical analysis

Measurements were carried out for two purposes. In the first place, specific measurements were used in an attempt to differentiate between species, type and sex. For example, metrical analysis of sheep/goat metapodia and calcanea was carried out to try to distinguish between the species. Specific measurements of sheep scapulae were taken to try to establish whether long- or short- tailed types were present on the site. Measurements of the metacarpi of cattle attempted to differentiate between cows and steers. Secondly, general measurements were taken in order to assess the size and quality of the stock animals and to note any improvements during the periods involved. The key to the measurements taken appears in Appendix 1. Tables were compiled of the sample size, range, mean, standard deviation and coefficient of variation for each measurement in all periods. Where possible measurements were compared to those from other contemporary sites in order to observe any variations between different regions. Many of the measurements correspond to those described by von den Driesch (1976) and can be compared directly with other European faunal assemblages.

Butchery practices

Any cut marks discovered on bones and any recurrent breaking points were noted. From these observations it was possible to draw some conclusions about butchery practices. It was possible, for instance, to discover in what way the carcass of a particular animal was divided up into joints and how certain bones, horns and antlers were used in the production of tools and ornaments. The study of the proportions of the various categories of bone represented in each species also provided information about butchery practice in the periods concerned.

Skeletal abnormalities

Note was taken about any bone that had suffered a trauma or had been affected by disease. Certain congenital factors were also observed and are discussed in the appropriate section.

The strands of evidence discussed above were drawn together in an attempt to obtain a clear idea of how each species was exploited and how this exploitation varied during the 1,800 years of occupation under consideration. The recent series of excavations in Exeter has recovered one of the largest and best preserved faunal samples from an urban site in Britain. The analysis that follows inevitably raises as many questions as it solves but these are questions that will be answered by further work on faunal samples from other contemporary urban or rural sites. It is still true to say, however, that the animal bones from Exeter present an invaluable opportunity to examine the animal exploitation of a regional centre in the Roman and succeeding periods. In the following chapters I will endeavour to make the most of this opportunity.

2.

THE QUANTITATIVE ANALYSIS

The purpose of this chapter is to study in detail the results of the quantitative analyses for the Roman, medieval and postmedieval periods in turn, in order to observe the changes and trends that were taking place.

In the consideration of the data from these periods, it is tempting simply to compare the relative percentages of the species present in the various phases without regard to any variations in the types of bone fragments encountered. However, such a method of analysis is too simplistic. It cannot be assumed that the faunal sample from Exeter, despite its large size, represents, in any phase, a cross-section of the animal bones deposited in the town at the time. Accordingly, it is hazardous to compare results from different phases without first considering the types of bone fragments present in the samples, since variations in these may influence the relative percentages obtained for each species. Therefore, in order to make valid comparisons between samples of different dates, it has first to be established that the samples under consideration are statistically similar in their constituent parts.

The following analysis therefore also endeavours to test whether the quantitative methods usually employed on archaeological faunal material are adequate for complex sites. As a result, the study of the samples from many of the phases is of a lengthy and detailed nature. Space precludes the publication of all the data on which the results are based but summaries of the number of fragments of each species and the minimum number of individuals represented are given for each phase. Where the samples are of sufficient size, the proportion of fragments and the proportion of the sum of the minimum numbers (S.M.) within each of the seven bone categories (as described on page 7) are given for cattle, sheep/goat and pig. The analysis is published in full to aid comparisons with other sites and to act as the basis for future work in Exeter itself. Some may not wish to study the results in their full detail and accordingly a discussion and summary of the conclusions are given for each major period at the end of the relevant section. The chapter ends with a discussion of the methodology of quantification in the light of this study and the general conclusions that can be made about the animals represented in Exeter.

THE ROMAN PERIOD

The subdivision of the sample

The total number of bone fragments examined from the eight sites with Roman material amounted to 18,317 of which 9,730 were identifiable. The sample was subdivided into the following nine groups:

R1) The period of military occupation (approximately 55 to 75 A. D.).

R2) The late first century (approximately 75 to 100).
R3) Features dated to 55 to 100.
R4) Features dated to the late first-early second centuries (approximately 75 to 150).
R5) The second century (100 to 200).
R6) The third century (200 to 300).
R7) Features dated to the second and third centuries (100 to 300)
R8) The fourth century until the end of the Roman occupation (300 and after).
R9) Undated Roman features.

It was possible to subdivide the sample into smaller units in the first place the dating evidence was not precise enough and some of the rubbish layers may have accumulated over a considerable period of time; secondly further subdivision would have made many more of the samples too small to be statistically significant. The number of fragments and the minimum number of individuals for phases R3, R4, R7 and R9 are included in Table 6 but the number of fragments found was insufficient for any assessment of a more detailed nature to be worthwhile. Tables 1 to 6 include all the fragments recovered from the various Roman deposits. The presence of any burial or burials is marked in the table by an asterisk and the number of fragments involved is given in the footnote to the table. The tables do not take into account variations observed in the Roman samples and it is these that need to be considered in depth.

The individual phases

R1 — Features dated to the period of military occupation (approximately 55 to 75 A. D.)

Material was recovered from the GS, TS, RS and Cathedral Close (MM/CC) sites (Figure 1). The GS and TS sites were partially occupied by barrack blocks during this phase and the Cathedral Close sited included material associated with the building of the legionary baths. Consequently, this gave an opportunity to compare the bone assemblages from sites of quite different natures during the period of occupation by the Roman forces.

2,717 animal bone fragments were examined, of which 1,321 were identifiable. 96% of the identified mammalian fragments from all the sites belonged to cattle, sheep/goat and pig (Table 1). The identified fragments of the principal stock animals were subdivided into seven bone categories and the results are shown in Table 7 for the GS, TS and MM/CC sites. The sample from the RS site was too small for detailed analysis. It can be seen that cattle fragments were more abundant on the GS site, in which they contributed 48.89% of the fragments of the principal stock animals. This figure, however, was inflated by concentrations of skull, jaw and loose teeth fragments (Category 1) in GS F.49 (cobbles), F60 (road level) and L.424 (floor makeup). Including these features the proportion of Category 1 fragments (0.44) was much higher than on other sites dated to this phase. Even when these features were excluded, the proportion of Category 1 fragments (0.39) was high compared to most other Roman samples (Table 8). The GS cattle sample therefore differed substantially from the smaller TS and MM/CC samples and this appears to have had a direct bearing on the proportions of fragments represented (Table 7).

The sheep/goat and pig assemblages also displayed lateral variation in their contents. The samples of sheep/goat from the GS and MM/CC sites were quite similar but the small and possibly unrepresentative TS sample had significantly higher proportions of tibia, radius and ulna fragments (Category 3 = 0.41, Table 7). Pig was better represented on the MM/CC site (30.88%) than on the others, a trend that continued in most subsequent Roman phases. It is interesting to note that the proportion of pig Category 1 fragments (0.58) in the GS sample was the highest of all the Roman samples. The same is true of the sheep/goat sample (0.32). These correlate with the higher concentration of cattle skull, jaw and teeth fragments in the same deposits. There is a possibility that these bones, which have relatively little food value, were dumped together during the disposal of carcass waste, perhaps in association with the provisioning of the troops living in the barrack blocks nearby.

R2 — Features dated to the late first century (approximately 75 to 100 A.D.)

Five sites (GS, TS, MM/CC, RS and HL) produced animal bone dated to this phase. The Cathedral Close site (MM/CC) included material associated with the modification of the Bath House after the departure of the legionary forces, and with dumps of furnace ash (Bidwell 1979). The RS material was all obtained from RS F. 363. This was the defensive ditch of the legionary fortress and was deliberately infilled during this phase with debris that included large amounts of animal bone. The other sites were residential areas within the Roman town.

3,697 animal bone fragments, of which 2,018 were identifiable, were examined. About half of these came from RS F. 363 and comparatively large samples were obtained from the GS and MM/CC sites. The TS and HL sites produced very small quantities of bone. Fragments from the principal stock animals contributed 93.68% of the identified mammalian fragments (Table 2).

A more detailed study of the material revealed the outstanding example of inter-site variation discovered in the Exeter animal bone assemblages. The sample from RS. F.363 included 1,036 identifiable mammalian fragments, 754 of these belonged to cattle, 157 to sheep/goat, 51 to pig, 57 to horse, eleven to dog, four to roe deer and two to red deer. A minimum number of 49 cattle was established from the mandible fragments. A minimum of fifteen sheep/goat (radius), five pig (teeth) and four horse (teeth) were also represented (Table 2). The concentration of cattle fragments in this ditch was such that they contributed 78.38% of the principal stock animal fragments — a much higher percentage than in the great majority of the Roman deposits (Table 7). The cattle sample was dominated by jaw, skull and loose teeth fragments, as the extremely high proportion of Category 1 fragments (0.72) demonstrates.

In addition 86 metatarsi and 26 metacarpi fragments were recovered, giving a proportion of 0.15 for the Category 4 fragments (metapodia). Several of the metatarsi had knife cuts just beneath the proximal epiphysis where they had been detached from the rest of the carcass. In stark contrast, very few good cattle meat bones were recovered — a fact clearly demonstrated by the extremely low proportions of fragments belonging to Categories 2 and 3 (Table 7). Another interesting aspect of the sample was the almost complete absence of horn cores, despite the abundance of other skull fragments. There seems no doubt that this assemblage represents evidence of the primary butchery of cattle carcasses, in which their heads and other unwanted portions of their bodies were discarded. The good meat bones were taken elsewhere for marketing and the horns were probably required for the manufacture of tools and ornaments. The proportion of cattle phalanges was relatively low (Category 6 = 0.02) and it seems likely that these were also taken elsewhere, either for food or in the manufacture of glue. However, the possibility that poor preservation conditions contributed to the low representation of these fragile bones cannot be ruled out. The concentration of this material suggests that either many cattle were being slaughtered nearby or, at least, that the material from the primary butchery process was brought to the ditch during the deliberate infilling that took place in the late first century.

The sheep/goat and pig assemblages did not display the same trends as the cattle remains in RS F. 363, perhaps indicating that their carcasses were treated in a different manner. It should be noted, however, that over half of the 51 pig fragments recovered belonged to Category 1 and once again correlated with the concentration of cattle skull and jaw fragments. The sample was nevertheless heavily biased in favour of cattle and this made direct comparisons with the relative proportions of animals on other sites meaningless.

The number of pig fragments on the MM/CC site was swollen by the presence of three partially surviving burials of young animals, which contributed 70 fragments (Table 2). All three were very young and may have died of disease. They were certainly not butchered for food and were discarded from the subsequent analysis.

Excluding these burials, the proportions of the principal stock fragments were more typical of the rest of the Roman deposits on both the GS and MM/CC sites. Once again, however, their constituent parts were significantly different. The proportion of the carpals, tarsals and phalanges (Categories 5 and 6) was substantially greater on the MM/CC site for all the principal stock animals. The number of pig metapodial fragments was also much higher on that site (Table 7). These discrepancies (the causes of which will be discussed later) meant that, although the proportion of stock animals represented was similar, the samples from which the results were obtained were significantly different.

Of the remaining mammalian species, only horse contributed over 1% of the identified fragments. This was due entirely to the concentration of skull and jaw fragments in RS F. 363 dumped together with the more numerous cattle waste bones. Red deer, roe deer, hare and dog fragments were present in small numbers. Eight fragments from a skeleton of a fox were discovered on the GS site.

R3 — Features dated from approximately 55 to 100 A.D.

Only 69 fragments from the RS and HL sites were examined from this phase, which contained features not specifically datable to phases R1 and R2. Details of the

11

species represented are given in Table 6 but the numbers involved were too small for further analysis.

R4 — Features dated from approximately 75 to 150 A.D.

66 fragments from the TS site were dated to this phase which overlaps with phases R2 and R5. Details of the species identified are given in Table 6.

R5 — Features dated to the second century

Seven sites produced animal bone from this phase. All were basically residential areas during this time except for the MM/CC site, on which the town's Basilica was situated. Of these sites, four (RS, HS, HL and BS) contained too little bone for detailed analysis. The majority of material was recovered from the Guildhall sites (GS and TS) and a total of 3,680 fragments was recovered from all deposits dated to this phase. Of these 1,992 were identifiable (Table 3).

Table 7 again shows the inter-site variations encountered among the principal stock animal fragments. Employing a simple count of fragments, cattle varied between 28-49%, sheep/goat 32-40% and pig 19-34% on the GS, TS and MM/CC sites. The cattle assemblages on the GS and TS sites were very similar, although both contained higher proportions of Category 3 fragments than any of the other Roman deposits. This was in stark contrast with the MM/CC site, in which the fragments of radius, ulna and tibia made up only about 6% of the cattle sample. On that site also, as in the previous phases, the proportions of Categories 5 and 6 (0.09 and 0.16 respectively) were high. The sample also contained the lowest proportion of Category 1 (0.20) and the highest proportion of Category 2 (0.39) fragments in any of the Roman cattle assemblages.

The sheep/goat samples showed some similar traits. The GS and TS sites both had relatively high proportions of Category 3 fragments but the GS site produced an unusually low proportion (0.19) of Category 2 bones. The MM/CC sample differed from the other two in the high proportions of Categories 5 and 6 (0.07 and 0.07 respectively) and the highest proportion of Category 2 fragments (0.39) found in the Roman deposits.

The percentage of pig fragments was higher on the MM/CC site and this again correlates with the unusually large number of phalanges (0.11) and metapodials on this site.

The GS and TS deposits were both associated with residential areas. No heavy concentrations of cattle skull and jaw fragments were found in features associated with them and it is reasonable to assume that most of the bone was deposited as kitchen waste. The variations between these sites and those of the MM/CC site were marked and consistent for all the stock animals and probably reflect both differential preservation conditions and marketing practices.

None of the remaining mammalian species, which contributed only 3.12% of the identified fragments, were important in the diet. The species identified were horse, hare, red deer, roe deer, dog and cat (Table 3).

R6 — Features dated to the third century

Material was examined from the TS, MM/CC, RS, HL, BS and HS sites but only the sample from the MM/CC site was large enough for statistical analysis. 874 of the 1,293 fragments dated to this phase were found on that site (Table 40).

The number of cattle fragments on the Cathedral Close (MM/CC) site was inflated by the concentration of skull fragments in some of the features and also resulted in a high proportion of Category 1 fragments (0.47). Generally, however, the cattle sample displayed the same characteristics as others from the earlier phases of this site. Both the cattle and sheep/goat assemblages contained high proportions of Categories 5 and 6. The pig sample was heavily weighted by fragments of metapodials (Category 4 = 0.27) and phalanges (Category 6 = 0.19), as Table 7 demonstrates. This concentration of these bones was even more pronounced than in the other phases of the MM/CC site. In several cases the bones of individual trotters were found in close association and were obviously thrown away together. Their presence sets the MM/CC assemblage apart from the other Roman samples.

Red deer, roe deer, hare, dog, cat and badger provided 14.86% of the identifiable mammalian fragments. These included bones from three burials. 42 fragments of badger and 23 of dog survived from two burials in the MM/CC deposits. Fifteen of the hare fragments from the TS site belonged to one individual (Table 4).

R7 — Features dated 100 to 300 A.D.

Only 77 fragments from features on the RS site belonged to this phase. Only cattle, sheep/goat and pig were identified and the sample was too small for further study (Table 6).

R8 — Features dated to the fourth century and later (300 A.D. and after)

The largest sample of Roman animal bones was collected from deposits dated to the fourth and early fifth centuries. Four sites (GS, TS, MM/CC and RS) produced material from this phase. The nature of occupation on the Guildhall sites (GS and TS) had changed by this time. The building plots previously occupied by several houses were amalgamated and replaced by large stone town-houses. One of these was associated with a farmyard and stock enclosure, from which a lot of animal bone was recovered. The TS site was occupied by two yards. One was covered with a thick loamy deposit, which has been interpreted as mud and dung accumulated whilst cattle were kept there. Ditches found on the adjoining GS site are in turn interpreted as cattle enclosures or droveways. The fourth century MM animal bone material continued to show similarities with that of previous phases. A midden, possibly dating to the early fifth century (CC L.14) was of a different nature, however, and was treated separately in the following analysis.

5,794 fragments from all sites were examined. Over 3,500 of these were found in the GS deposits mostly in ditches. Over 1,400 were found in layers on the TS site and about 500 in deposits on the Cathedral Close site. Cattle, sheep/goat and pig provided 95.38% of the identifiable mammalian fragments (Table 5).

Examination of the principal stock fragments again revealed evidence of the concentrated disposal of cattle skull and jaw fragments on the GS site. Nearly half of the cattle fragments belonged to Category 1 (0.49). The high percentage of cattle fragments (54.85%) was a direct reflection of the concentration of this skull material on this site (Table 7). The sheep/goat and pig samples were more typical of other Roman deposits. The cattle skull and jaw material was not, however, evenly scattered throughout the GS deposits. Instead certain sections of the ditches (GS F.47, F.160, F. 618) contained concentrations of such material. When these sections were excluded from the analysis (Table 8), the proportion of cattle Category 1 fragments fell sharply to 0.26 and was more typical of other Roman deposits. The proportion of cattle fragments

(43.81%) also decreased. The nature of the sheep/goat and pig samples remained virtually unchanged. The slaughter and primary butchery of cattle possibly kept in the adjoining farmyard may well be associated with these concentrations of cattle waste bones among ordinary domestic refuse.

All the layers on the TS site produced consistent collections of animal bone Cattle dominated the assemblage contributing 71.48% of the principal stock fragments. Such a high percentage could not in this instance be attributed to concentrations of Category 1 fragments (0.36). The types of bone represented from all the principal stock animals were similar to others associated with domestic refuse deposits. The preservation and recovery of these bones was as good as most of the other Roman samples and the increase in the percentage of cattle fragments cannot be attributed to those factors. It is tempting to correlate the increase with the presence of the cattleyard on the site, although the causes of such an interaction are not obvious.

The sample from the fourth century MM deposits was small but it continued to show concentrations of pig metapodials and phalanges of all the principal stock animals and contained a much higher percentage of pig fragments than other samples dated to this phase (Table 7). The late Roman midden (CC L.14) produced over 70% cattle fragments in its sample of 135 identifiable principal stock fragments. The proportion of cattle fragments was similar to that of the TS site, although the sample was too small to be very reliable.

The fourth and fifth century deposits therefore continued to reveal the complexities of faunal material from urban sites. Lateral variations caused by differential disposal of bone elements and possibly by the change in function of a site were again recognisable and had a significant bearing on the proportion of the species represented.

Of the remaining mammalian material, small quantities of bone belonging to red deer, roe deer, hare, horse, dog, cat, fox, hedgehog and woodmouse were recovered. None of the species played an important role in the diet.

R9 — Undated Roman features

1,147 undated Roman fragments were examined from the GS site. Because of the lack of close dating no further analysis of the material was worthwhile. Details of the fragments recovered are given in Table 6.

Lateral variation in the Roman deposits

The Roman samples were taken from areas of different functions and should be expected to produce pronounced variations in their faunal remains. Some of these variations were found consistently on a particular site. The Cathedral Close site (MM/CC) provided the best example of this. Apart from the midden dated possibly to the fifth century, these deposits were characterised by the large number of phalanges of all species, a high proportion of pig metapodials, generally a low proportion of Category 1 fragments and a higher proportion of good meat bones of all species. The percentage of pig fragments recovered from this site was consistently higher than on any of the others (Table 7).

Several factors could lie behind these trends. The occurrence of the smaller bones in larger numbers — particularly the sheep/goat and pig phalanges — could be the result of more careful excavation of this site than others in Exeter, in which more may have been overlooked. This, however, appears unlikely since the standard of excavation on the Cathedral Close site differed little from the others.

A second possibility is that the preservation of the bone on the Cathedral Close site was substantially better than on the other sites and thus more bones of smaller volume and density survived. This again would favour the recovery of the phalanges in particular, which have very low densities and are very susceptible to destruction (Binford and Bertram 1977:109). It is certainly true to say that the preservation of bone on this site was excellent and significantly better than much of the material from the GS, TS and RS sites. A study of the survival patterns of the articular surfaces of the long bones of the principal stock animals supports this. The ends of the long bones contain a high proportion of spongy cancellous bone, which is more vulnerable to destruction than the cortical bone of the shafts. This applies particularly when the cancellous bone is directly exposed. Unfused or butchered epiphyses are therefore less likely to survive. The proportion of unfused and fused epiphyses of the same fusion age was fairly consistent for all the principal stock species throughout the Roman deposits. The ratio of articular surfaces to shaft fragments varied significantly however. Assuming that the fragmentation of the bone is constant, the ratio of shaft fragments should be higher in poorly preserved deposits, in which a greater proportion of articular ends have been destroyed. To take the tibia as an example, the ratios of the articular surfaces to shaft fragments in the Cathedral Close deposits (excluding the fifth century midden) were 1.63:1, 1:1.57 and 1.50:1 for sheep/goat, cattle and pig respectively. From the rest of the Roman deposits the equivalent ratios were 1:2.57, 1:2.89 and 1:1.38. Restricting this analysis to the later-fusing and more vulnerable proximal tibia, the ratios of articular surfaces to shaft fragments were 1:1.93, 1:5.50 and 1:2.50 for sheep/goat, cattle and pig respectively on the Cathedral Close site and 1:16.27, 1:8.53 and 1:3.38 elsewhere. Similar variations in these ratios were found in the humerus, radius and femur. In all cases the articular surfaces of these long bones were found more commonly on the Cathedral Close site than on the other Roman sites. Using such ratios as a rough guide and assuming that differential fragmentation did not play an important role, it seems clear that the more fragile bones had a better chance of survival on the Cathedral Close site. The higher proportions of Category 2 bones in the MM/CC deposits and the abundance of phalanges and other vulnerable bones can therefore be attributed to some degree to differential preservation.

This factor alone cannot, however, explain all the discrepancies in the Cathedral Close assemblages. In particular, the concentrations of pig metapodial fragments were not the result entirely of the excellent preservation of the bones on that site. Such high proportions of these bones are more likely to have been the result of differential disposal patterns on the Roman sites. Pigs' trotters are a recognised cut of meat in modern times but this may not have been the case in the Roman period. The concentration of pig metapodials and phalanges, sometimes from the same foot, and the lack of butchery marks on these (although they require little) suggest that these were often thrown away whole and not regarded as a source of meat. The same explanation may apply for the concentrations of cattle phalanges and sheep/goat tarsals and phalanges, although preservation conditions also aided their survival. The proximity of the Cathedral Close deposits to the Forum — the marketplace of the Roman *civitas* — cannot be overlooked. Some carcass trimming is to be expected at such a distribution centre and it is possible that the unwanted feet of the major food animals were cut off and dumped nearby. Good meat bones were discovered in the same deposits and there is no doubt that the Cathedral Close site contained a large amount of kitchen waste as well.

From the archaeozoological point of view, the animal bones from the ditch RS F. 363 represent the most important material discovered in any of the periods investigated at Exeter. They provide clear evidence of the slaughtering and marketing techniques practised on cattle in the early Roman period. The contents of the excavated sections of the ditch have already been discussed in detail (see section R2). The interpretation is of great interest. The cattle bones deposited represent the parts of the carcass considered to be of no further use. Consequently very few meat bones were found and mandibles, skull fragments and metapodia dominated the sample. Yet, virtually no horn cores were discovered. The recovery of sawn and chopped horn cores elsewhere in the Roman deposits strongly suggests that these were detached from the rest of the skull to utilise the horn sheath in the manufacture of artifacts or ornaments. Also, despite the large number of metapodia fragments, relatively few phalanges were recovered from the ditch (despite the sieving of some of the layers). The discovery of concentrations of these on the Cathedral Close site indicates that these were often taken elsewhere after the initial butchery of the carcass. The overall impression of the RS F. 363 material is one of a consistent and extensive exploitation of the cattle carcases for distribution in the town.

In comparison, the concentrations of skull and jaw fragments in the ditches of fourth century date on the GS site represent primary butchery on a much smaller scale. Certainly, the number of skulls and jaws in certain sections of the ditches witness a similar type of disposal of waste bones but these were interspersed by sections that contained material more typical of the domestic refuse deposits elsewhere in the Roman town. Whether these concentrations of skull material can be linked directly to the stock enclosures that appeared on the adjoining TS site or not, it is possible to postulate that the slaughter of cattle was carried out in a much more decentralised pattern in the later Roman period. Clearly the evidence is as yet far from conclusive but such an hypothesis would fit in with the archaeological evidence. The presence of a Roman garrison in Exeter between approximately 55 and 75 A.D. entailed the provisioning of about 6,000 men in addition to the needs of the civilian inhabitants. It is likely, therefore, that the organisation of the food supply was of paramount importance in the early years of the town. The animal bones from the Rack Street ditch are in levels that postdate the departure of the legionary forces but belong to a period when direct Roman influence was still important. The large-scale, organised and systematic slaughtering, butchery and distribution of cattle carcasses, which these deposits evidence, are practices likely to have been inherited from the period of military occupation.

The social structure within the town had changed by the fourth century, as witnessed by the construction of large stone town-houses on the Guildhall sites on plots of land previously occupied by several houses (Bidwell *pers. comm.*). At least one of these, as we have seen, was associated with its own farmyard and stock enclosure. It seems likely too that the stock brought there was slaughtered for consumption in the town. If this was a pattern that was followed elsewhere in the town and its hinterland, it is possible to visualise a much more decentralised system of cattle slaughtering and marketing, mainly in the hands of large stockowners who managed their own animals independently. It has been shown at the Roman villa at Gatcombe that the slaughter and butchery of the estate's

stock took place there and much of the meat was taken away for marketing elsewhere (Branigan 1977: 201). Such a system of distribution may have been typical of the economic and social organisation elsewhere in the later Romano-British period. The region around Exeter is unusual in its lack of villas but it is possible that a similar system was operating in the area. The evidence of stock enclosures associated with the slaughter of cattle in the Exeter deposits may therefore represent the urban counterparts of the marketing processes on the rural estates elsewhere in Roman Britain. Such changes need not have affected the sale of meat from the market place, as the continued evidence of carcass trimming from the Cathedral Close deposits may imply. Future research will no doubt shed further light on this topic.

Relative abundance of species in the Roman deposits

Most of the previous discussion has centred upon the lateral variations of bone within the Roman deposits. These provide important insights into aspects of the economy of Exeter but cause many problems in the interpretation of the relative importance of the various species in the meat diet. It has been shown that the various stages in the butchery process can affect the relative number of fragments of the principal stock animals recovered. It is also obvious that none of the samples in the Roman phases needs represent a cross-section of the animal bones deposited in the town. Comparisons between phases therefore should be limited to samples which contain similar types of bone.

Accordingly, samples biased by the concentration of cattle skull and jaw fragments dumped in the primary butchery process have to be excluded from an overall analysis. Most of the remaining animal bone assemblages have been interpreted as domestic waste and, in theory, can be directly compared. Table 8 is an amended version of Table 7, listing the number of fragments of each of the principal stock animals and their category proportions excluding the deposits most heavily biased by concentrations of primary butchery material. Chi-square tests were employed on each sample to establish whether the proportion of fragments in each of the seven categories was similar to that of the cumulative total of all the Roman deposits for cattle, sheep/goat and pig in turn. Table 8 shows that about half of the samples tested were significantly different from the overall totals. These tests, unsophisticated as they are, can be used in this way to act as a quick guide to the similarity of various samples. In this case it is apparent that the amount of inter-site variation was such that changes in the relative percentage of fragments of the principal stock animals may be a function of sample variation rather than changes in the relative importance of the stock in the meat diet. Any direct comparisons may therefore be misleading.

Similar statistical tests can be made on the minimum numbers represented by each bone. This drastically reduces the sample size for analysis. Accordingly, the minimum numbers of the various bones within the seven categories were added together to obtain the 'sum of minimum numbers' (S.M.). Most of the resulting samples were now of sufficient size for simple statistical tests. Table 9 lists the minimum numbers, the S.M. and the category proportions of each of the principal stock animals. The chi-square tests revealed that the samples bore a much greater degree of similarity using this method of analysis. All the cattle samples were statistically similar to the overall category proportions and only one of the pig and three of the sheep/goat samples were significantly different at the 1% level of chi-squared. The reasons for the decrease

Cat was the only one of the rarer mammals represented in any numbers (21 fragments from four individuals). The high number of fish fragments (116) on the GS I-II site was principally the result of a concentration of these in GS F. 114 (Table 23).

Md6 — Features dated to the late thirteenth century

This phase produced the second largest sample of bones from the Exeter excavations. 10,313 fragments were recovered, of which 5,692 were identifiable. The GS III site itself provided 6,800 of these fragments, while the GS I-II site contributed over 2,000 and the TS site over 1,400. Some of the 39 deposits contained a large number of fragments; most contained over 100, and several produced over 500. Cattle, sheep/goat and pig, as usual, completely dominated the assemblage and accounted for 95.54% of the total number of identifiable mammalian fragments (Table 26).

Unfortunately, as was the case with the largest medieval sample (Md2), the deposits dated to this phase produced significant inter-site variations, making an overall comparison employing the fragments method of counting once again impossible. All three principal species were affected.

The cattle assemblage showed the least variation. Only the GS I-II sample was found to be significantly different at the 5% level of chi-squared. The GS III and TS sites produced very similar category proportions in their cattle samples (Table 27). Within both sites, however, there was a fair degree of variation between features, although no clear pattern was discernable. The cause of divergence in the GS I-II sample cannot be ascribed to a single deposit. The intra-site variations met on this site were generally no greater than those encountered on the other two. Overall, there was a higher proportion of Categories 1 and 3 cattle fragments on the GS I-II site than on either the GS II or TS sites, with a a correspondingly smaller proportion of Category 5 (carpals and tarsals) fragments.

The caprine assemblage too showed bias. The TS sample was found to be significantly different at the 1% level of chi-squared. The reasons for this were a low proportion of Category 1 fragments (0.15) and a high proportion of Category 3 fragments (0.35). Once again this trend was evidenced in most of the features on the TS site and not in just one or two isolated deposits, although a few features did emphasise the trend more than others.

Finally, the pig sample was biased by the high proportion of Category 1 fragments (0.54) on the GS I site and by the extremely variable amounts of Category 3 fragments found on the three sites in question (0.09 to 0.32). Both the smaller GS I-II and TS sample showed significant variation at the 1% level of chi-squared. Once more the observed variations were not the product of one or two atypical deposits.

Although the percentage obtained from a simple count of fragments varied by only 3 to 7% for the principal stock animals in this phase on the three sites in question, sample variability precluded any direct comparisons between them.

In this phase not even the minimum numbers method was able to nullify all the inter-site variability. The pig sample on the GS I-II site was still significantly different at the 5% level of chi-squared, due to the variations in the proportions of Categories 1,3 and 4 (Table 28). The minimum number of ten pigs on that site was obtained from the teeth. The second most represented bone was the femur (eight) and that bone is probably a better indicator of the proportion of pig on that site, since the high figure obtained for the teeth

reflects the bias in the sample towards Category 1 bones (0.36). This would cause the percentages of stock animals on the GS I-II site to be amended as follows: sheep/goat 44.18%, cattle 37.20%. pig 18.60%, in a total sample of 43 individuals. The variations observed in the proportion of the seven bone categories in the other two species were still quite large but the smaller numbers involved in the S.M. method meant that none of the variations was significant. Sheep/goat continued to dominate the assemblage, contributing 44 to 53% of the stock animals on the three sites, with an amended average percentage of 48.30%. Cattle were second (average 31.40%) and pig last (average 20.29%). Once again these percentages have close similarities to the previous four phases, although this does not take into account sample variance between them. It is of interest to note that the lateral variations found in the assemblages of all three principal species during this phase were caused by similar phenomena. The GS I-II site had higher proportions of Category 1 fragments for all three species than the other two sites, although the trend was more marked with pig than cattle or sheep/goat. Both the pig and sheep/goat samples on the TS site were found to have much smaller quantities of Category 1 bones and unusually high concentrations of Category 3 fragments. These variations could again be explained simply in terms of differential butchery practice, in which the GS I-II site was subject to a higher proportion of waste fragments being dumped in its deposits. Certainly the variations cannot be explained in terms of differential preservation or recovery, since the proportions of the smallest and most fragile bones represented on the three sites were found to be consistent.

92 fragments of cat were recovered from the late thirteenth century phase (2.17%). These fragments belonged to at least sixteen individuals (6.40%). None of the other mammals present attained levels of over 1% of the fragments, although hare was a little more common than usual (0.87%). Rabbit still appeared extremely rarely and only six fragments of deer were identified. Horse as always appeared rarely in deposits derived mainly from food refuse. Thirteen of the twenty dog fragments came from one burial and in fact a minimum of only three dogs was present (Table 26).

Md7 — Features dated from 1200 to 1300

Only three features, all from GS III, were dated to this phase. In all 141 fragments were recovered and 61 identified. The sample was too small for detailed analysis to be worthwhile (Table 29).

Md8 — Features dated to the late thirteenth to early fourteenth centuries

1,038 bone fragments were recovered from five features on the GS I-II and GS III sites. 535 of these were identifiable. The percentage of cattle, sheep/goat and pig in the mammalian sample was 96.55% (Table 30).

The chi-square tests upon the cattle and sheep/goat samples revealed no significant bias in the deposits. The number of pig fragments was too small for such calculations to be made. The cattle sample showed a fair degree of variation, especially in the proportions of fragments in Categories 1 and 4, but relatively few fragments involved meant that the difference between the GS I-II and GS III sites could still be ascribed to chance. Both the sheep/goat samples had high proportions of Category 1 fragments (0.33 and 0.36) and low proportions of Category 2 fragments (0.18 and 0.20). Because of these unusual category proportions, the percentages of the major stock animals recorded in this phase (54.14% sheep/goat, 33.33% cattle, 12.53% pig) could not be directly compared with any of the other phases (Table 31).

A minimum number of only 24 individuals could be assigned to this phase, and the numbers involved precluded any significance tests being carried out on the category proportions of the principal species. Overall the percentages of 50% sheep/goat, 29.17% cattle and 20.83% pig were similar to those of the preceding phases, but the sample was small and the proportions of the sheep/goat assemblage were such that any conclusions must remain tentative (Table 32).

Of the other mammalian species only cat, dog, horse and hare were present in these deposits, all in small numbers (Table 30).

Md9 — Features dated to the early fourteenth century

Eleven features from the GS I-II, GS III and TS sites contributed 2,145 fragments, of which 1,237 were identifiable. All the 459 fragments from the GS III site were discovered in one deposit (F. 296). The five GS I-II features contributed about half the fragments dated to this phase. The principal domestic stock accounted for 95.22% of the 1,005 identifiable mammalian fragments (Table 33).

Chi-square tests were again carried out where possible on the principal stock assemblages and these showed no significant lateral variation in the fragments represented in the cattle and sheep/goat samples. The pig sample was again too small for such tests to be carried out. However, despite the homogeneity of the sample, the percentages obtained for the stock animals on the three sites varied a lot. The GS III sample in particular was unusual in that only 33 fragments of cattle (21.85%) were recovered. This was even less than those of pig (23.18%). In contrast, on the GS I-II site, cattle contributed 50.60% of the fragments. In the phase as a whole, cattle and sheep/goat contributed about 43% of the stock fragments (Table 34). The variations in the percentage of fragments on the sites are probably the result of the small sample sizes from a limited number of features dated to this phase.

The chi-square tests on the S.M. also showed no significant variation in the cattle and sheep/goat assemblages. The bones from which the minimum numbers of each species were calculated on the three sites in question were generally typical for the animals involved (Table 35). The minimum numbers method of counting also eradicated most of the lateral variations in stock percentage figures encountered in the count of fragments. In a sample of 65 animals, sheep/goat contributed 56.92% of the individuals, cattle 27.69% and pig 15.38%. The percentages on each site varied by about 6 to 7% for sheep/goat and cattle and about 2% for pig. The GS III site, which produced the highest percentage of sheep/goat should be treated with suspicion since the sample was taken from only one feature.

The representation of the remainder of the mammalian sample was typical of the medieval period. Cat was the most common of the rarer mammals, contributing 2.09% of the mammalian fragments (Table 33). Horse, hare, dog (whose seven fragments all came from one skeleton) red deer and rabbit were also occasionally represented.

Md10 — Features dated to the late fourteenth to fifteenth centuries

Features dated to the period immediately subsequent to the Black Death unfortunately did not contain enough faunal material to indicate what effect the plague had, if any, on the diet of the inhabitants of Exeter. Only 795 fragments

from fourteen features were analysed, of which 479 were identifiable. The GS I-II and TS sites between them contributed all but five of the fragments dated to this phase. 93.69% of the fragments belonged to the principal stock animals (Table 36).

In this phase, chi-square tests were only feasible on the sheep/goat sample and these indicated no significant variation between the GS I-II and TS sites, although the variation in the number of fragments in the seven bone categories was quite high. The TS site contained a high proportion of sheep/goat Category 1 fragments (0.42). In addition 17 of the 37 pig fragments (0.47) dated to this phase also came from the skull or jaw. Consequently, the overall percentages of 47.16% sheep/goat, 39.72% cattle and 13.12% pig are best kept in isolation, since the assemblages are different in content to those of other phases (Table 37).

In a sample of only 33 individuals, any assessment of the relative percentages of stock obtained through the minimum numbers method in this phase is a hazardous procedure and the results given in Table 38 should not necessarily be considered representative.

Of the rarer mammals, cat, hare, horse, dog and rabbit were represented in small numbers. 108 of the 112 fish fragments recorded from the TS site were recovered from TS F. 169 and that concentration accounted for the large percentage of fish on that site (Table 36).

Lateral variation in the medieval deposits

The detailed examination of the medieval deposits again revealed the effects of lateral variation in animal bone assemblages even from neighbouring sites. The variability encountered was less dramatic than in the Roman deposits. No large scale dumps of material associated with the primary butchery process were discovered, for example. This is not surprising as the majority of the bone was derived from domestic rubbish and cess pits. If large scale dumping of particular parts of the carcases took place in this period, the evidence for it is unlikely to be contained in these deposits. Smaller concentrations of particular bone types were encountered, however. The abundance of sheep and goat horn cores in the GS I-II deposits of twelfth century date (Md2) may be associated with the manufacture of horn objects, for example. In several instances concentrations of skull and jaw fragments of one species coincided with those of one or more of the others. Similarly, unusually large numbers of good quality meat bones were found sometimes in the assemblages of all the principal stock animals in the same deposits. In addition, there was often a positive correlation between the proportions of carpals, tarsals (Category 5) and phalanges (Category 6) represented.

Several factors could account for the inter-site variations observed in these deposits. Differential preservation of bone is one, although there was no consistent evidence of this from the observations of the condition of the surviving fragments. Some waterlogged pits, which produced large concentrations of fish in some instances, did preserve more of the fragile bones but there was no consistent inter-site variability. Differential recovery is another factor that can influence the types of bone represented. The increase of Category 5 and Category 6 bones in some deposits is probably indicative of both good preservation and recovery. Again, however, these variations were not confined to one site and cannot explain other aspects of lateral variation. It is also possible that the inter-site variations reflect the different social status or wealth of the inhabitants of the various sites. Such a phenomenon was not reflected, however, in the pottery types (Allan *pers. comm.*) and the best cuts of meat (represented by Category 2 bones in particular) showed no consistent trend to be more common on a particular site. Indeed, there is no reason why variability in social status should be reflected in this way.

Despite the variability in the assemblages, there seems no doubt that all parts of the skeleton were liable to be deposited in domestic rubbish deposits. This could imply two things: the first is that the householders themselves did a lot of their own butchery of carcases; the second is that they procured from the market (or other source) all parts of the skeleton, even the portions that have little food value. Given adequate space and by salting the meat, there is no reason why individual households could not store complete carcases on occasions for domestic consumption. However, it is necessary to compare these assemblages with those of other sites in medieval Exeter before such distributions can be better understood.

Relative number of animals represented in the medieval deposits

Since the analysis was confined to a large sample of bone obtained from one area of the town, it is theoretically possible to obtain some idea of the relative abundance of the domestic species, whose meat was consumed by the inhabitants of that neighbourhood. Such a premise does not take into account several factors. The first is that the abundance of material was concentrated mostly in features dated to the twelfth and thirteenth centuries. Evidence from the late medieval period was extremely limited due to the change in disposal practices, which resulted in the digging of much fewer refuse pits in the areas in question. Secondly, it is possible that the evidence from these pits is not representative of all the disposal practices. Some bones may have been cast onto the ground surface where they are more likely to have been destroyed. There is no guarantee that these bones were the same types as those that were dumped in the pits. Thirdly, it has been shown that inter-site variability still played an important part in the relative abundance of the species represented. This meant that some of the methodologies usually employed in quantitative analysis of animal bones were inadequate for such a complex situation.

The complexity of the deposits and the variations encountered between individual features, sites and phases meant that the method of counting all the identifiable fragments could not be employed as an accurate means of comparing the relative number of stock animals in the medieval period. Because different concentrations of bone types can affect the relative number of fragments represented, direct comparison between two phases can only be made in cases where the samples of all species are of a similar nature, and in practice these were found to be comparatively rare.

Other faunal analysts have counted individual teeth and skull fragments separately from the rest of the sample, no doubt in recognition of the fact that these fragments in particular are subject to a great deal of variability in archaeological samples, since often a large concentration of loose teeth and skull fragments may represent the smashed remains of relatively few jaws and skulls. Certainly many of the biases observed in the medieval phases of Exeter resulted partly from the variations in Category 1 fragments. However, these were not the only cause of the sample bias. When all Category 1 fragments were excluded from the medieval sample and a constant proportion for each of the

six remaining categories established for each species using data derived from the period as a whole, chi-square tests still revealed significant variations in the cattle and sheep/goat assemblages. Table 39 gives the results of these calculations. Pig was the only stock animal that was found to have an homogeneous sample in most of the phases. However, only the small Md10 sample showed no significant variation in the samples of all three species. The results of this analysis meant that it was not possible to compare the relative percentages of fragments found in the ten medieval phases, even after Category 1 fragments had been isolated from the rest of the samples.

The question must then be posed as to whether the minimum numbers method of counting is in fact a valid method of assessing the proportions of stock animals in this period, given the fact that the fragment samples were so heterogeneous in nature. As has been seen, the chi-square tests on the proportions of the sum of the minimum numbers in each bone category usually revealed less variation than that observed in the count of fragments. However, this in itself does not mean that the number of individuals calculated for a particular species was not biased by the inclusion of an atypical concentration of one type of bone. A case in point is the twelfth century (Md2) sample from the TS site. As was demonstrated above, although the significance tests on the cattle sample indicated that the contents of the various categories were similar to those from the other sites in that phase, the presence of an unusually large number of calcanea had raised the minimum number of cattle to a misleadingly high level. With this method, however, such discrepancies were easier to spot and overcome and although caution had still to be exercised the method was found to be much more reliable in a complex urban situation than the fragments method of counting. Its major drawback, however, was that except in the phases where an abundance of faunal material was recovered, the sample sizes of the minimum number of individuals obtained were small. As a result, although the general trends were apparent, any more subtle variations in the relative number of stock animals during the medieval period could not be recognised.

In order to test whether valid comparisons could be made between the various medieval phases using the minimum numbers method, an overall proportion for each of the seven categories was obtained for each species by adding together the sum of the minimum numbers obtained for the respective categories from all the deposits. Chi-square tests were then performed on each sample to test the null hypothesis that each sample was statistically similar to the medieval sample as a whole. In cases where the total sum of the minimum numbers was less than 40, the tests were not carried out, since the samples were too small for such tests to have much value.

The results of the analysis are given in Table 40. These showed that only three of the samples were biased at the 5% level of chi-squared: the cattle sample on the TS site in the Md1 phase; the sheep/goat sample on the GS I-II site during the Md2 phase; and the sheep/goat sample in the Md5 phase on the GS III site. None of the variations encountered in the other samples was found to be significant. The three biased samples did not unduly affect the relative percentages of the stock animals in their respective phases; but in order to obtain a statistically similar sample, the three sites involved were excluded from the calculations in those phases.

The resulting percentages of stock animals for all medieval

phases are shown in Table 41. The figures for the Md2 and Md6 phases were based on the amended number of cattle and pig individuals respectively. Caution should be maintained over the interpretation of the results from Md4, Md8 and Md10 phases, since these samples were fairly small. In general, however, the results do show a fairly consistent pattern (Figure 2). Sheep/goat was the most common species with percentages ranging from 44 to 57%. Cattle was the second ranked species with between 27 to 34% of the minimum number of individuals. Pig was third with percentages that varied between 15 and 23%. The variations in the percentage figures can be explained simply as the variations one would expect in samples of a relatively small size, although the figures possibly do suggest that sheep/goat did become slightly more important numerically in the thirteenth and fourteenth centuries but according to these figures there was no dramatic change in the relative numbers of stock animals deposited in those areas throughout the Middle Ages.

Calculations of the minimum amount of meat weight represented by these figures were made on the largest samples. As will be seen later, there was no dramatic improvement in the size of the animals during this period and accordingly the Roman estimates of meat weight, as employed in Table 10, were used again. The criticisms and problems which were cited for the equivalent Roman calculations should be remembered in this instance as well.

As expected in a period in which the relative proportions of animals remained relatively constant, a fairly stable picture emerges in this analysis as well. Cattle provided 73 to 78% of the meat, sheep/goat 12 to 19% and pig 8 to 12% in the phases involved (Table 42). Even allowing for substantial errors in the estimations of the sizes of the animals and in the relationship between the percentages obtained for the minimum number of individuals and the actual proportion of livestock on the sites, beef in its various forms remained by far the most common meat during the Middle Ages in Exeter.

THE POSTMEDIEVAL PERIOD

The subdivision of the sample

The postmedieval sample was of similar size to the Roman assemblage. 17,928 fragments were studied, of which 10,865 were identifiable. Over 80% of the remaining fragments belonged to ribs and vertebrae of domestic animals. The bones were subdivided into the following four groups:

Pm1) Features dated to the sixteenth century (1500 to 1600).

Pm2) Features dated to the late sixteenth - early seventeenth centuries (1550 to 1650).

Pm3) Features dated to the late seventeenth century (1660 to 1700).

Pm4) Features dated to the late seventeenth eighteenth centuries (1660 to 1800).

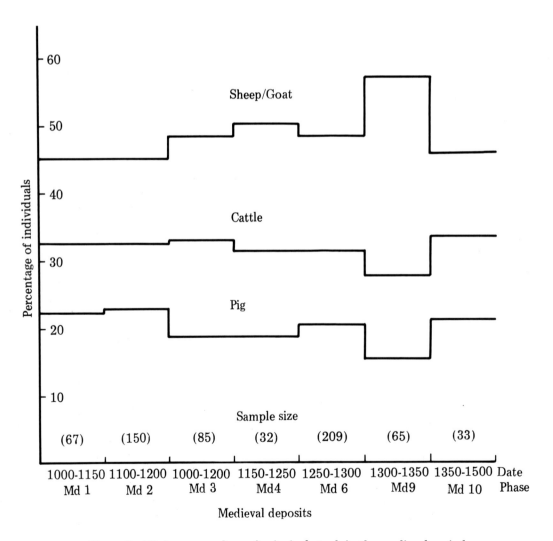

Figure 2 Minimum numbers of principal stock in the medieval period.

1,074, but by that time one of the manors had been leased out and the number of animals on its lands was not recorded (Finberg 1951:145). Unfortunately, similar figures were not quoted by Finberg for other stock animals, other than those obtained from Domesday Book, so it was not possible to compare the numbers of pigs and cattle with those of sheep, in order to establish whether there was any change in the relative numbers of stock kept on the estates during the medieval period. Such results would have proved interesting, although the same trends need not have been reflected in eastern Devon, where Exeter is situated.

One is therefore left with the Domesday record as the only detailed documentary source of livestock numbers in the medieval period. The information about the Domesday survey of Devon is extant not only in the Exchequer Book but also in another volume known as the 'Exon Domesday' which gives details of the survey in the counties of Cornwall, Devon and parts of Wiltshire, Somerset and Dorset (Trow-Smith 1957:66). A translation of the text was published in the Victoria County History of Devonshire in 1906 (Vol. 1 403-549). The following is a typical entry of a manor held in demesne to the King, the Church and other landowners:

'Ruald has a manor called Wenforda (Wonford) which Edmer held T.R.E. (in the time of King Edward) and it paid geld for ½ virgate. This 2 ploughs can till. Walter de Osmundvil holds it for Ruald. Of this W(alter) has in demesne 1 ferding and 1 plough and the villeins 1 ferding and 1 plough. There W(alter) has 2 villeins, 2 serfs, 20 beasts, 8 swine, 30 sheep, 10 goats, coppice 1 furlong long by ½ furlong broad, 50 acres of meadow and 2 furlongs of pasture taking length and breadth. Worth 15 shillings a year; when R(uald) received it it was worth 5 shillings'. (Page 1906:510).

Such records therefore give quite detailed information about the amounts and types of land owned, the number of animals kept, and the number of villeins and serfs on each manor. The references to livestock concern the actual numbers of animals recorded and also the animals that pulled the ploughs. It is generally assumed that the plough-team consisted of eight cattle, although one or two discrepancies in the Domesday text may indicate a six-beast team. On one manor in the vicinity of Exeter, however, (Creedy Peyherin), it is recorded in the Exon Domesday that the villeins possessed one plough and had seven oxen towards another. In the Exchequer version the same manor is recorded as having two complete ploughs (Page 1906:482-3). Accordingly it seems that eight-beast teams were the usual complement. Therefore in the quoted example the two ploughs mentioned would indicate that sixteen cattle were kept for such purposes on those lands. Horses were not employed in ploughing in Devon until much later times.

The twenty beasts (*animalia*) also recorded on the Wonford estate are usually assumed to be non-ploughing cattle. This would bring the quota of cattle on that manor to 36. Occasionally cows (*vaccae*) were recorded but never on the same holding of land as *animalia*. The *animalia* may have consisted mainly of breeding stock, which would have been required to replace with new stock the oldest members of the plough team when their working days were over. However, it is doubtful that the number of *animalia* recorded for Devon as a whole (7,357) would have been sufficient to have provided all the replacements required for the 46,066 cattle in the 5,758¼ plough teams unless the average working life of plough animals was an extremely long one. It is possible that only adult animals were recorded.

Alternatively some of the breeding herd may have been included in the numbers of the plough team. The question cannot be answered satisfactorily from historical records alone.

Another problem encountered with regard to the total number of cattle in Devon at the time is the fact that in the Domesday Book a total of 90 entries, which were recorded as possessing plough lands, did not mention the presence of any plough teams (Welldon Finn 1967:245). Most of those lands, however, consisted of fairly small tracts which may not have had much, if any, ploughing done on them.

Bearing these factors in mind, the total numbers of livestock on demesne lands in Devonshire in 1086 is recorded in Table 56. If the numbers of the principal stock animals are considered alone, the relative percentages read: sheep/goat 48.57%, cattle 45.28% and pig 6.16%. The numbers of pig are certainly under-represented since there are several instances of manors where swineherds were recorded as paying an annual rent to the landowner but no pigs were actually mentioned. In Devon as a whole 264 swineherds paid 1,343½ pigs in rent, while 110 others were not stated to pay any fixed sum (Trow-Smith 1957:80).

The animals listed for Devonshire, assuming that all were utilised for food upon their deaths, would have gone to other markets as well as Exeter and the picture for the county as a whole may not reflect the situation in the vicinity of the city itself. Accordingly, only the manors in the surrounding area of Exeter were considered (Figure 3). Livestock in the reduced area would still have found other markets, such as Crediton, but the results ought to give a better indication of the resources available to Exeter. Table 56 shows that on the demesne lands in the Hundreds around Exeter cattle and sheep/goat were recorded in almost equal numbers (48.69% and 49.22% repectively). The very low percentage of pig (2.09%) is misleading since in this area 49 swineherds are recorded as paying 253 swine yearly and another five swineherds paid 31s. 3d/ annum to their respective landowners .

Can such figures be used in a direct comparison with the animal bones recovered from Exeter? It is unfortunate that one cannot be certain that either source of evidence is an accurate reflection of the relative numbers of livestock kept in the area. Domesday Book only records animals held on demesne lands. It does not take into account the livestock owned by villeins and serfs on holdings that were not subject to the Domesday assessment. How large a proportion of the total stock this entailed is impossible to say but it cannot be assumed that the ratios of the stock animals on the demesne lands were the same as those on other holdings. The poorer peasant, if he had any livestock at all, would tend to keep pigs and sheep, which are less costly to maintain than cattle. If this was the case, the relative percentages of cattle and sheep/goat may in fact be somewhat biased in favour of cattle but to what extent is unknown. Nor do the records state whether all animals of a species were recorded Young animals are nowhere specifically mentioned and it is possible they were not included in the accounts. Nor indeed need the population of Exeter have consumed a true cross-section of the meat available to them in the surrounding countryside. As will be discussed in Chapters 3 and 4, it is possible to argue a case that many older cattle and sheep/goat did not find a market in the city. In addition the two methods of counting employed may not accurately reflect the true ratio of the species being brought into Exeter.

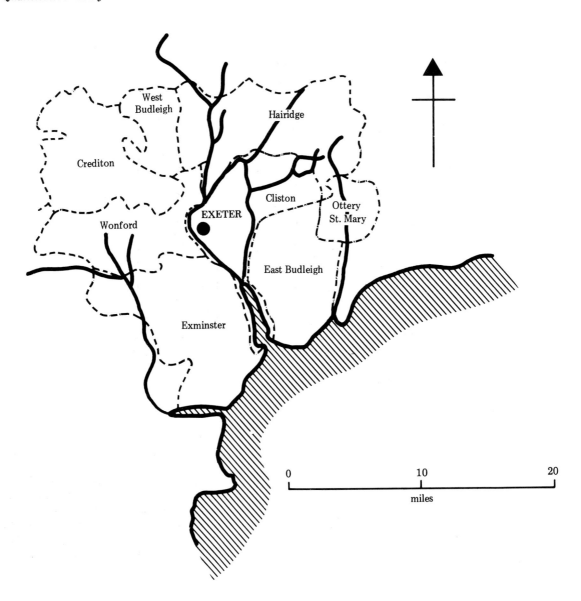

Figure 3   The Hundreds around Exeter.

An equally important point is that, whereas Domesday Book records living animals, the analysis of animal bones attempts to estimate the proportions of the animals slaughtered. They are therefore dealing with quite different phenomena. It will be shown later that many of the sheep/goat represented in the early medieval layers of Exeter were immature animals whereas the majority of the cattle were mature. Assuming for the moment that the animals represented in Exeter were a cross-section of the animals bred in the surrounding area, cattle in terms of absolute livestock numbers kept are probably underestimated in the archaeological samples because of their longer life expectancy.

Consequently, when the relative percentages of sheep/goat and cattle recorded in the demesne lands around the town are compared with the data obtained from the two methods of counting the bone fragments in the excavations, the results have to be treated with suspicion, since the results obtained from all three methods may not be indicative of the actual percentage of livestock numbers in the area. Figure 4 shows the relative percentages of cattle and sheep/goat obtained from the three sets of analysis. Pig was excluded from the comparisons because of its obvious under-representation in the historical records. The data of

the minimum numbers were taken from the GS I-II and GS III sites in deposits dated to the eleventh and early twelfth centuries (the Md1 phase). The percentage of fragments was calculated from data obtained from the largest of the Md1 samples, that of the GS III site. The results revealed that the variations in the percentage of animals obtained by the three methods were in the order of about 14% and that the results from the Domesday survey (49.7% cattle) lay between the two extremes obtained from the fragments method of counting (about 56% cattle) and the minimum numbers method (about 42% cattle). The results therefore showed general similarities but it is not possible to draw direct comparisons because of the quality of the data involved.

The results of the quantitative analysis of the Exeter faunal material must in some ways remain largely inconclusive. It is apparent that the traditional methodologies used in such analyses have to be improved. Large samples from well excavated urban sites will be understood fully only by detailed statistical examination of the individual fragments. As the number of variables considered increases, the only practicable way to study the material is through the use of multivariate analysis. Such techniques are useful only in large samples, however, but more limited statistical technique

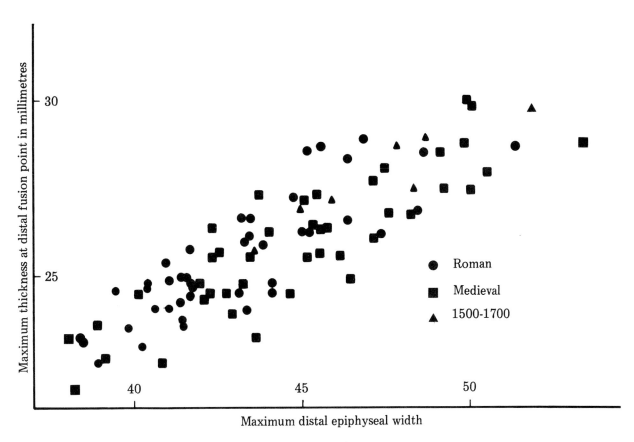

Figure 9   Scatter diagram of cattle metatarsi measurements.

Not only were there larger specimens at Alcester but also the average size of the specimens was consistently greater. A comparison of the absolute size of cattle can be made by multiplying the lengths of complete long bones by a constant factor to obtain an estimation of withers height. Using Fock's conversion factors for the metapodia (von den Driesch and Boessneck 1974:336), the mean of the various calculations made on the Roman metapodia from Exeter ranged between about 107 to 111 cm. In the late Roman levels at Alcester the same calculations ranged between about 114 and 115 cm. The estimation of withers height obtained from medieval specimens at Exeter showed no improvement in the size of the stock. The various estimates ranged between about 104 to 108 cm based again on relatively small samples. No detailed comparisons from contemporary medieval sites are available at the time of writing. A large sample of Saxon material from Southampton (Hamwih) has produced mean withers heights of about 115 to 117 cm from the complete metapodia (Bourdillon and Coy *in press*). It seems possible, therefore, that the overall size of the cattle brought to Exeter in the Roman and medieval periods was smaller than in other parts of the country.Assuming that the majority of the stock was reared in Devon, it may be possible to discern regional variations in stock size during these periods. Whether the variations were due to differences in the types of animals bred or in their planes of nutrition remains for future research to determine.

By the postmedieval period, movements of cattle across the British Isles became widespread (Skeel 1926) and stock management improved. Both factors lie behind the improvement in the size of cattle brought to the Exeter market in that period.

THE TYPES OF CATTLE REPRESENTED

Several attempts have been made to analyse and interpret

the morphological and metrical characteristics of horn cores from British archaeological sites. Two medieval horners' deposits at Coventry and at York have been studied in detail. Both sites produced several types of horn cores. At Coventry four types were distinguished from a sample of 37 horn cores, which the author implied may have been indicative of different types of cattle (Chaplin 1971:138-42). Four types were also recognised in a sample of 175 horn cores from Petergate, York but Ryder (1970) concluded that the animals were all of a similar type.

Recently a series of detailed articles concerning the craniology of cattle has been published (Grigson 1974; 1975; 1976; 1978). It has been demonstrated that the measurements of the circumference of the base of the horn core and its overall length show significant sexual dimorphism within a breed. It was also shown that the growth rate of horn cores is high during the first two years of the animal's life and thereafter diminishes rapidly to a new low growth rate which is maintained until the animal is about seven years old (Grigson 1974:366). There is therefore a problem in using such data on archaeological material, since it is usually impossible to age the horn cores that are recovered. It is likely, however, that the sample from Exeter derives mostly from adult animals, judging from the ageing data.

A detailed system for the classification of horn cores from archaeological sites has also been devised (Armitage and Clutton-Brock 1976). The criteria involved include size, curvature, torsion and the shape of the cross-section. By first dividing the horn cores by size into 'small horned', 'short horned', 'medium horned' and 'long horned', the sex of the core is designated by the study of its morphological characteristics. The terms 'short horned', etc. are descriptions merely of size and not of breed or type of cattle.

31 Roman and 107 medieval horn cores were examined from the Exeter excavations. Table 67 summarises the metrical analysis of the basal circumference and the length along the outer curvature of the cores. The great majority fell into the 'short horned' category. These possessed basically an ovoid cross-section, although there were variants in which the cross-section had a more flattened or more rounded appearance. This variability is caused to some extent by sexual dimorphism (Armitage and Clutton-Brock 1976:332). The anterior edge of the horn core base usually formed an angle of about 100 to 110° with the frontal bone. Most cores then gradually arched forward and narrowed fairly uniformly but quite sharply towards the tip. At the same time many of the horn cores curved gently upwards from the frontal profile often forming an angle of 25 to 35° with its junction with the skull. There was a lot of variation in the relationship between the length of the horn cores and their basal circumference. Generally, however, the latter measurement was a few millimetres longer than the former. Indeed many of the cores were similar to the 'short horned' group of Roman specimens from Angel Court, London, illustrated by Armitage and Clutton-Brock (1976:338).

Athough sexing of each individual core was not possible, few had the characteristics of bulls and the majority were similar to those of castrates and cows, although the distinction between these was not always clear cut.

The smallest cores fell into the 'small horned' category but were similar in many respects to those described above. These tended to curve upwards much more sharply, usually at an angle of over 50°. It is possible that these belonged to younger animals whose horn cores were not fully developed. Certainly they do not resemble the small cores commonly found on iron age sites and their tendency to appear more porous than the majority of horn cores suggests that they are simply younger specimens of the same type. A few cores were substantially different from the majority. Two medieval specimens (belonging to the few that fell into the 'medium horned' range) had very round cross-sections and were very long in relation to their basal circumference. These morphological characteristics suggest that they belonged to cows, possibly of a larger type of cattle than was usual. One example of a naturally polled animal was discovered in a twelfth century deposit.

Animal bone remains can rarely be used to differentiate between breeds of cattle. Indeed breeds as we know them today were probably not differentiated until the later post-medieval period. The concept of breeds also relies on factors such as the colour of coat, which cannot be determined from osteological evidence. Broad classes of animal can be seen, however. Examination of the Exeter horn cores demonstrated that most animals were of the 'short horned' type. There was no evidence of 'long horned' cores in these periods. Such cores have been recovered from fifteenth century deposits at Baynard's Castle, London (Armitage and Clutton-Brock 1976:330). Documentary evidence on the types of medieval cattle is virtually non-existent. Traditionally the Red Devon breed is considered to have been prominent in the area in the later postmedieval period and has been thought to have had a long heritage in the area. They were considered as excellent draught animals (Thirsk 1967b:186). Scale models of this breed made by Garrard at the end of the eighteenth century showed oxen and cows which had shoulder heights of approximately 112 to 121 cm (Clutton-Brock 1976:21-22). Great play has been made of the recording of the acquisition of a 'red heriot' at Tavistock Abbey in 1366 (Finberg 1951:133). Trow-Smith has suggested that the heavy concentration of cattle in North

Devon, as recorded in Domesday Book, could indicate the beginnings of a slow expansion of the Red Devon breed (Trow-Smith 1957:85). However, the documentary evidence on this point is somewhat equivocal. There is evidence that in the middle of the eighteenth century the majority of cattle in Devon were in fact black (Stanes 1969). Clearly the animal bones from Exeter do not shed much light on this problem. It can be said, however, that the cattle in the area during Roman and medieval times were probably of a similar type of animal of a size possibly smaller than in some other areas of England at that time. The postmedieval period saw an improvement in the size and a greater concentration in the selective breeding of cattle which culminated in the appearance of modern breeds.

BUTCHERY AND MARKETING OF CATTLE

Butchery marks, fragmentation and the distribution of the fragments of different parts of the body were all taken into consideration in this analysis. What follows is a general summary of this evidence.

The skull and jaws

The concentrations of cattle skull and jaw fragments have been discussed in the previous chapter (pages 11, 14). Organised dumping on a large scale was found in the late first century levels of the legionary ditch (RS F. 363). Skull and jaw fragments together with bones of the limb extremities were found almost to the exclusion of the major meat bearing bones. Similar concentrations of skull and jaw fragments were found in the fourth century ditches on the GS site. Both deposits demonstrate the primary butchery process of cattle, in which the unwanted portions of the body were thrown away while the remainder of the carcases were made available for distribution or sale within the Roman town. The RS ditch deposit shows that a systematic policy for the marketing of beef was taking place in the first century. This does not mean that all cattle were butchered in the same way, however, as the presence of skull and jaw fragments amongst major meat bearing bones throughout the other Roman deposits indicates.

Similar large scale dumps of skulls were not discovered in the the medieval deposits, although several pits did have unusually high proportions of these bones. Certain postmedieval pits contained a large number of jaw and skull fragments of young animals. The majority of these samples came from only one area of the town and the lack of such concentrations of waste bones need not preclude the continuation of the practice elsewhere in the town. The archaeological evidence supports this theory. The proportion of cattle skull and jaw fragments in the medieval deposits was consistently lower than in the majority of Roman deposits, indicating that much of this material may have been dumped elsewhere.

The presence of skull and jaw fragments amongst ordinary domestic refuse in the deposits of all periods shows that the majority of the carcass was utilised commonly for food. Indeed the fragmentary condition of much of the skull material probably indicates that the skulls were often smashed to remove the brain. Similarly, butchery marks were found on the mandibles, particularly around the dorsal condyle at the back of the jaw and probably made to detach the mandible from the skull and enable the tongue to be removed easily.

The virtual absence of horn cores from the major Roman dumps of cattle skulls implies that cattle horns were required elsewhere for some industrial practice. Three small cores discovered in other Roman deposits had been sawn off about 40 to 60 mm above the base, a process which would have damaged the horn sheath and a practice that suggests that in some cases only the tip of the horn was required for working. More commonly, however, the Roman horn cores had been detached from the skull just below their base so that the whole of the horn could be utilised. This too was the common practice in medieval times. One skull of early twelfth century date bore evidence of cutmarks on the nuchal eminence just below the junction with both horn cores. In this instance they had not been detached but most medieval horn cores were cut from the skull at this point. A recent discovery of debris from a horner's workshop in another part of the city (Henderson *pers. comm.*) demonstrates that the horns of cattle were required as industrial raw material. Similar workshops have been discovered in Coventry (Chaplin 1971:138-142) and York (Ryder 1970). The evidence from Exeter suggests that this type of industry was already in existence in Roman times.

The long bones

The long bones bore the greatest evidence of butchery. Throughout the deposits less than 1% of the humeri, radii, tibiae and femora fragments had both epiphyses present (Table 68). Even allowing for the fact that many of these breakages could have occurred during or after dumping, most of them must have resulted from butchery for meat and marrow. Cutmarks were discovered quite commonly on these bones. To consider the fore limb first, this was detached from the rest of the carcass usually at the distal end of the scapula. This bone was often found to be broken near the point where the spine of the bone begins. Few cutmarks were actually found on the glenoid itself, where the scapula articulates with the proximal epiphysis of the humerus. The most common portion of the humerus to survive was the distal epiphysis and the lower end of the shaft. The knife cuts on this part of the bone and especially on the distal articulation were the result of cutting the meat off the bone rather than of the severance of the limbs. The main severance points appear to have been higher up the bone on the shaft, although some chop marks were found on the distal epiphysis itself. The proximal epiphysis of the humerus has a poor survival on archaeological sites and an insufficient number of these was recovered for conclusions to be made about this area of the carcass. Knife cuts corresponding to those on the distal humerus were found on the proximal portions of the radius and ulna in all periods. These were made during the removal of meat from the elbow joint. The radius was commonly broken or severed transversely both across the middle of the shaft and especially a little above the distal epiphysis, probably for the removal of marrow.

A similar picture of intensive butchery was apparent on the major meat bones of the hind limb. The proximal articulation of the femur commonly revealed butchery marks. These would have been caused by the same process that resulted in the marks often found on, or near, the acetabulum of the pelvis, with which the proximal femur articulates, when the hind limb was severed from the hip. The distal epiphysis of the femur was also a common area for knife cuts and in some cases, severing. The tibiae were always in a very fragmentary condition — not one from any period was intact — and breakages and cut marks were liable to occur anywhere along the shaft, although the mid-shaft and distal parts of the bone were the commonest areas for these.

As is to be expected, the major meat bearing bones were intensively butchered. Usually they were severed in several

places for the removal of marrow. The presence of so many of these bones amongst Roman and medieval domestic refuse suggests that meat was sold or distributed on the bone and that filleting of meat was not practised to a great extent. This may have become more fashionable in the postmedieval period, although there is little evidence of this from the present archaeological material.

The metapodia, tarsals and phalanges

The metapodia were comparatively more complete than the other long bones but still about 90% of them were found in a fragmented condition (Table 68). In the Roman deposits, several of the metatarsi in RS F. 363 had knife cuts on the posterior aspect of the proximal epiphysis made when the bone was detached from the tarsals. The majority of the metapodia were also severed midway down the shaft, probably for the removal of marrow. This section of ditch was unusual in that it contained many more proximal than distal epiphyses of cattle metapodia in its debris. 50 proximal epiphyses of metatarsi were discovered compared to only eight distal epiphyses. Usually the numbers of proximal and distal epiphyses of the metapodia were roughly equal in the deposits. The concentration of the proximal metapodia together with the discarded skull and jaw fragments suggests that these too were dumped during the primary butchery process of cattle. It also indicates that the distal half of the bones was required for some other purpose, possibly as raw material in the manufacture of tools or ornaments.

The metapodia of all periods were often severed laterally across the shaft, more often towards the distal epiphyses. Very few were split longitudinally. These bones have much less meat value than the other limb bones but contain a lot of marrow, which could be extracted by such butchery methods.

The tarsals also displayed evidence of knife cuts and chop marks on occasions. The calcaneum and astragalus often formed a severance point between the main meat bones and the extremities of the hind limb. Consquently they were sometimes chopped during the butchery process to facilitate this operation.

The phalanges have little meat value but can be boiled up in the manufacture of glue. Their low representation in many deposits can be explained both by their poor preservation and by their being overlooked during excavation. Their comparatively low representation in RS F. 363, however, included sieved deposits. Phalanges were not dumped necessarily during the primary butchery process in Roman times and their use in glue manufacture may have been the reason for this. Butchery marks on phalanges were rare in any period.

Ribs and vertebrae

Cutmarks were also present on cattle ribs and vertebrae. The practice of splitting the vertebrae down their dorso-ventral axis was uncommon before the postmedieval period when it became the established practice. Prior to that time, the vertebrae were more often found to be cut laterally. The change in this practice probably indicates that by the sixteenth century it was common policy to butcher the carcass into sides of beef. Before that date, the trunk of the body must have been cut laterally along the flanks of the animal.

The butchery and marketing of cattle carcases was obviously intensive. The overriding impression of the Roman and medieval cattle assemblages is that very little of the animal's skeleton was considered to be waste material. The parts of the animal of little or no food value were often utilised for other purposes such as tool manufacture, marrow extraction and possibly glue manufacture. The deposits produced evidence of large scale organised marketing of cattle in the early Roman period. Excavation of the areas of the city where the medieval and postmedieval butchers operated would no doubt produce a similar picture of organised butchery of carcases in those periods. Finds of leather from the medieval and postmedieval deposits have yet to be studied, but it must be remembered that the hides of cattle were an important part of the animals' market value.

SKELETAL ABNORMALITIES

The majority of the bone fragments produced no evidence of pathology. This may imply that the majority of animals were healthy when slaughtered, although many diseases do not affect the bone formation at all.

There were five instances where the second premolar of the mandible was absent. Three of these were of Roman date whilst the others were found in medieval deposits. A recent discussion of this condition has concluded that it was quite commonly found among both 'wild' and 'domestic' ruminants, and it has been put forward that such an absence is due to congenital factors (Andrews and Noddle 1975). Another phenomenon noted by Andrews and Noddle (1975: 140) was the absence of the fifth column of the third permanent molars on one of the cattle mandibles they investigated. Ten of the 76 mandibles with the M3 fully erupted from the Roman levels of Exeter had only, at most, the vestigial remains of the most posterior column present. Once again congenital factors are possibly the cause of this feature. It is interesting to note that this phenomenon did not occur in the large sample of medieval mandibles investigated at Exeter, nor has it occurred on any other sites of this date to my knowledge. Several Roman and Saxon sites, on the other hand, have produced mandibles with similar features. It seems as though this characteristic disappeared in England sometime after the Roman period. One Roman mandible had evidence for the overcrowding of teeth, the fourth premolar being set at an angle of 45° to the tooth row, a deformity that may have resulted from poor nutrition. Several less serious cases of malocclusion of the cheek tooth row were discovered in Roman and medieval samples.

One Roman and four medieval first phalanges had abnormal growths of bone around the proximal epiphysis. The proximal epiphysis of a seventeenth century metatarsus suffered from a condition which may have been caused by arthropathy or arthritis. Only one instance of a fractured bone was discovered: a 'cow-sized' rib of Roman origin had been broken at some stage of the animal's life and an irregular growth of bone formed over the fracture giving the bone a distorted appearance. It is unlikely that many casualty or diseased animals would have found a market in the city. Unless their carcases were transported to the town, which does not seem to have been a common practice in the Roman and medieval periods at least, the animals in question were probably not strong enough to be brought any distance on the hoof to the market, where in any case they may have been rejected or have fetched only a low price.

SUMMARY: THE EXPLOITATION OF CATTLE

Throughout the Roman and medieval periods the percentage of adult cattle eaten in Exeter was high and it seems that the majority of the stock was valued more for draught and dairy purposes. It is difficult to say whether cows were allowed to reach maturity principally for their milking, breeding or working qualities, or for a combination of these reasons. Documentary evidence would imply that, in the early medieval period at least, cattle were considered principally as draught animals. In the Roman period, however, there is some evidence to suggest that there was a greater emphasis on the keeping of mature cows rather than steers which may imply that dairy produce was a more important factor in cattle husbandry at that time.

In the medieval period the rates of immature slaughter continued at a low level, although there may have been some increase in the number of adolescent animals brought to the city in the later Middle Ages. It was not until the sixteenth century, however, that veal became an important food resource. The Exeter sample was biased by the inclusion of an unusually high number of very young jaws and bones in certain deposits, but the documentary and archaeological evidence both suggest that the raising of beef cattle had become an integral part of the rural economy. The production of veal was closely associated with dairy farming as documentary evidence makes clear.

There is no evidence before the postmedieval period of any attempt to improve the size of cattle in the area, which appears to have produced smaller animals than some other parts of the country. It was only when the raising and marketing of cattle became more commercialised and improved methods of grazing, fattening and eventually selective breeeding took place that any improvement was shown.

In the Roman and medieval periods it seems that most, if not all, of the cattle were brought to the city on the hoof for slaughter. Organised butchery of cattle carcases was a feature of the Roman deposits. No such centres for slaughter were found in the later deposits but such centres would have existed in other parts of the town where butchers slaughtered their animals. The postmedieval period brought a change in butchery practice in that the carcases were predominantly butchered into sides of beef and much fewer skull and jaw bones of adult animals were found amongst domestic rubbish indicating that many more of these were discarded at slaughter.

4.

THE EXPLOITATION OF SHEEP / GOAT

PROPORTION OF SHEEP TO GOAT

Horn cores

Although it is very difficult to differentiate between these species from osteological analysis, certain parts of the skeleton do display some diagnostic differences. Sheep horn cores, for example, can be differentiated from goat on the basis of shape. The former are roughly D-shaped in section and curved. Goat horn cores, on the other hand, are oval in cross-section and rise more vertically from the skull. Of the sixteen horn cores recovered in the Roman levels, ten could be assigned to sheep and the other six to goat. In the medieval deposits of the TS and HS sites, on which the most detailed analysis of horn core fragments took place, 63 specimens could be assigned to sheep and only 24 to goat. In addition, there were three sheep skulls which possessed no horns at all.

Metacarpi

Various attempts have been made to distinguish between sheep and goat by means of metrical analysis of the metapodia. One method is to measure the diameter of the medial and lateral articular surfaces of the condyles on the fused distal epiphyses of the bones and express the outer measurements as a percentage of the inner. The percentage is lower in goat than in sheep, the division being given at 62-63% (Boessneck et al. 1964:115-116). The indices of the maximum proximal width: maximum length, and the maximum distal width: maximum length were also calculated where possible. The metapodia of sheep are more slender than those of goat, although there is some degree of overlap (Boessneck 1969:354). Both methods were carried out on the metacarpi of all periods. In the Roman deposits measurements were only possible from five metacarpi. Four of the specimens produced distal condyle values ranging above 66%; the other produced a figure of 59%. It can be suggested that this bone belonged to a goat, whereas the others were from sheep.

In the medieval period, sheep metacarpi greatly outnumbered those of goat. In a sample of 45 distal epiphyses, upon which it was possible to take measurements of the condyles, only four could be ascribed to goat, whereas the remainder belonged to sheep. In addition, when the proximal and distal widths of six other metacarpi were compared to their greatest lengths, it was found that all six bones were slender enough to be classified as sheep. The two complete goat metacarpi possessed noticeably wider epiphyses in relation to their length than any of the complete sheep metacarpi.

In the postmedieval period none of the 41 fused metacarpi analysed could be assigned to goat. The ratio of the outer to inner condyle of sheep increased to over 70% in some cases. Many sheep metacarpi were much stouter in this period — a fact evidenced by the higher proportions attained by the indices of the proximal and distal widths: maximum length.

Metatarsi

An identical series of measurements was carried out for the metatarsi found in the deposits. In the Roman period, five of the eight specimens examined had distal condyle values of over 62% for both condyles, while the other three had values of 59 to 62%. When the proximal and distal width indices were calculated, however, they showed little difference between specimens with values of over 62% and those below it. This data combined with certain morphological criteria suggested that all the specimens belonged to one species, that of sheep.

Examination of 42 specimens of medieval date, using both methods of metrical analysis, indicated that only one bone certainly belonged to goat. This had condyle percentages of 57.6% and 57.8%, a proximal width: maximum length index of 0.17, and a distal width: maximum length index of 0.20. These indices confirm that the bone was stouter than the rest of the specimens, the majority of which had indices of 0.14 to 0.15 and 0.16 to 0.17 for the proximal and distal width indices respectively. The results therefore confirm the impression gained by the analysis of the metacarpi that the great majority of the caprine population brought to Exeter was sheep.

The results obtained from the postmedieval period are complicated by the fact that, like the metacarpi, the sheep metatarsi became relatively stouter. This makes the distinction between sheep and goat more difficult. One example had condyle percentages of over 63%, which would suggest that it belonged to a sheep, yet the proximal and distal width indices were 0.17 and 0.21 respectively, which meant that the bone was as stout as the goat identified in the medieval period. This was an extreme example, however, and most of the fourteen specimens, from which results were taken, could be assigned with confidence to sheep.

Calcanea

The maximum length of this bone is greater in goat than sheep in relation to its greatest width, although there are degrees of overlap (Boessneck 1969:352). Measurements on specimens from all periods in Exeter showed that the proportions between the two measurements were relatively consistent throughout and that most of the calcanea belonged to sheep. The dominance of sheep in the samples was also evident from the metrical analysis of the articular facet following the criteria of Boessneck *et al.* (1964:104).

Morphological observations

These observations supported the impression gained from the metrical analyses that the samples consisted principally of sheep. Certain diagnostic fragments (particularly the proximal femur, the radius and the third phalanx) occasionally possessed characteristics distinctive of goat but by far the majority could be positively identified as sheep.

Accordingly, the horn core evidence would suggest that a higher proportion of goat was exploited in Exeter than that of the long bones. The same discrepancy has been observed on other sites. At the iron age oppidum of Manching and on several Dutch sites of Roman date this was explained by the fact that, whereas all goats on the sites possessed horns, some sheep were hornless (Clason 1967:78). This probably accounts for some of the variation in the Exeter material, since polled sheep skulls were discovered, albeit in small numbers, in the medieval and postmedieval deposits. More important, however, was the use of horn for industrial manufacture. This may have favoured the recovery of goat horn cores, since their horns were larger in general than those of sheep and presumably were more in demand. Consequently, concentrations of horn cores found in some features on the Goldsmith Street site dated to the twelfth century may be misleading and biased in favour of goat. With regard to the metrical analysis, the results obtained from the metacarpus appear to be the most reliable, although it should be remembered that the results are limited to the fused specimens of animals over eighteen months old. The exploitation of sheep and goat may have been quite different and the proportions of sheep and goat amongst the unfused specimens may not have been the same. The results from the metacarpi indicate that in the medieval deposits less than 10% of the sample belonged to goat and that in the postmedieval period goat disappears almost entirely from the deposits. The other measurements and morphological criteria (employed on both young and old bones) support this view.

According to Domesday Book, there were on the demesne lands in the Hundreds around Exeter 1,613 goats compared to 9,689 sheep, a percentage of 14.27% of the total caprine stock (Table 56). This figure is similar to the results obtained from the twelfth century deposits in Exeter, in which three of the 30 fused metacarpi examined (10%) belonged to goat. The flimsy documentary evidence contains some evidence that goats became less common during the later Middle Ages: there is no mention of them in the account rolls of Tavistock Abbey in the fourteenth century and it seems that the Bishop of Exeter did not keep any goats on his estates either in 1328 (Finberg 1951:129). There is not as yet enough archaeological material dated to the fourteenth century in Exeter to confirm or deny this trend, although certainly by the sixteenth century, goats had become very scarce indeed inside the city. No goat bones were positively identified in the Plymouth sample of over 1,000 caprine fragments dated to the fifteenth century (Dennell *pers. comm.*).

AGEING DATA

The use of ageing data is limited by the fact that the jaws and long bones of sheep and goat are hard to differentiate in many cases. The tooth eruption data and fusion evidence of the two species cannot realistically be separated. It is possible that the exploitation pattern and mortality rates of sheep may have been radically different from those of goat. However, since sheep appear to have greatly

outnumbered goat in the deposits of all periods, it is possible to obtain a good indication of the mortality rates of sheep in samples of sufficient magnitude.

The methods employed and the problems encountered in the ageing of sheep and goat jaws have been discussed in Chapter 1 (page 7). With the exception of 40 mandibles of medieval date employed in a comparison of Carter's (1975) and Grant's (1975) methods of ageing mandibles, individual results from the 450 jaws examined are not given. Instead Tables 69, 72 and 76 summarise the data by giving details of the number of jaws that reached or failed to reach various stages in the tooth eruption sequence. The stages employed were:

> Stage 1 Both columns of the M1 in wear.
> Stage 2 Both columns of the M2 in wear.
> Stage 3 P4 in wear.
> Stage 4 All columns of the M3 in wear.
> Stage 5 M1 in heavy wear.
> Stage 6 M2 in heavy wear.

'Heavy wear' is defined as the stage beyond the relatively long-lasting 'mature wear' stage defined by Payne (1973: 288). That stage is equivalent to Stage g of the permanent mandibular molars in the system of tooth wear analysis devised by Grant (1975:439). A similar process occurs on the maxillary molars. The sequence of tooth eruption and wear is well defined but the absolute ageing of this sequence in Roman and medieval times is very much a problem. As in the case of cattle, improvements in husbandry during the last 200 years have increased the rate of tooth eruption, as data derived from eighteenth century 'semi-wild' hill sheep indicate (Silver 1969: 297). Even these figures are not reliable, since the ages cited for the eruption of some of the teeth by the eighteenth century sources do not correlate with the eruption sequences evidenced on British archaeological sites (Ewbank *et al.* 1964:423). Several ageing scales for sheep jaws have been used on British material in recent years based on estimates of Ewbank *et al.* (1964), Silver (1969), Payne (1973) and Carter (1975), all of which differ in detail. Tables 70, 73 and 77 follow the ageing scales employed by Carter but it should be emphasised that these figures are only estimates derived from archaeological interpretation. It has not been established from modern specimens that the rate of decline in height of the permanent molars due to wear (upon which the method is based) is in fact uniform, nor similar to that envisaged by Carter. The rate of tooth eruption is slower than that proposed by Ewbank *et al.* but may significantly underestimate the true age of the animals and should be treated as a guide only.

The Roman period

118 jaws of sheep/goat bore evidence of dentition. The specimens were subdivided into samples dating to A. D. 55 to 100, 100 to 300, and over 300. The results of the analysis are shown in Table 69. Throughout the Roman period at least two-thirds of the jaws belonged to animals that died prior to the completion of the tooth eruption sequence (Stage 4). Correspondingly high figures were obtained for Stages 1 to 3. The situation appears to have been fairly consistent in all the phases studied, with minor variations probably explained by small sample sizes obtained from some of these. Tables 69 and 70 show that the main peak of slaughter lay between Stages 2 and 3 (approximately 15 to 26 months). In all phases, however, a few specimens belonged to animals probably over four years of age and at least four examples belonged to senile animals, probably well over six years old.

The study of fusion data produced a number of problems of interpretation (Table 71). Sometimes epiphyses of the same fusion age gave contradictory results. For example, there were noticeably less unfused calcanea than unfused proximal epiphyses of femora. Yet both fuse at about 30 to 36 months, according to figures provided by Silver (1969:285-6). The most likely explanation of this discrepancy is that the unfused calcanea had less chance of survival and recovery than the larger bones such as the femora because of their small size and more delicate state: consequently they produced higher percentages of fused specimens than expected. The distal metacarpus and distal tibia also show incompatible results, although both epiphyses fuse between 18 to 24 months, according to Silver. For example, in the sample taken from deposits dated to the second and third centuries, all fourteen of the distal metacarpi were unfused but only 25 of the 48 distal tibiae were in a similar condition. It is probable that some of the metacarpi with fused distal epiphyses were employed in tool-making and consequently were missing from ordinary refuse deposits, biasing the remaining sample in favour of the unfused specimens. It is possible that the metatarsus was used in a similar fashion and this bone was also treated separately in the analysis. The preservation of the epiphyses of sheep/goat bones is linked to their age of fusion and to their specific gravity (Brain 1967; Binford and Bertram 1977). Table 71 (and also Tables 75 and 78) show that many more of the early fusing epiphyses were recovered than those which fuse later in the animal's life. This helps to explain some of the discrepancies in the results. It also serves to emphasise that the percentages of unfused specimens obtained by this method should be treated as relative figures only, since the samples are biased to an unknown degree in favour of the denser, fused epiphyses.

Despite these problems, there was a broad correlation between the two sets of ageing evidence. For example, according to the pooled data from the proximal humerus and tibia and the distal radius and femur, a consistently high percentage of epiphyses were unfused (about 61 to 70%) and belonged to animals that died before 36 to 42 months of age. The results also confirmed that the kill-off of young animals was quite high.

It is unfortunate that the period when the evidence from the jaws suggests that the most intensive slaughter took place (15 to 26 months) is covered mainly by fusion data from bones that appear to give misleading results, notably the phalanges and metacarpus. The distal tibia (18 to 24 months) gave a consistently lower figure of animals killed (22 to 25%) than that indicated by the tooth eruption data for that age, and in some cases a lower percentage than those given by epiphyses of earlier fusion ages. For some reason it seems that a greater percentage of unfused distal tibiae failed to survive. Certainly the small dimensions of many of the shaft fragments would suggest that a far greater percentage than about 25% was unfused. It is also possible that the epiphyses fused a little before the main period of slaughter of the stock.

Because of the doubts about the absolute ages of the animals, one cannot state categorically that the main slaughter of stock took place in the autumn or winter of the animal's second year, although this would have been one of the best times for such culling, since the sheep would have provided at least one fleece at this age and the slaughter of non-breeding animals at that time of the year would allow more pasture for the remaining stock.

The medieval period

In this period it was possible to make comparisons between the two methods of classifying and ageing teeth employed by Grant (1975) and Carter (1975). Grant's method of classifying sheep mandibles was identical to that employed on cattle. Each stage of the surface wear pattern of the M1-M3 was noted and a numerical value for the whole tooth row was obtained by adding up the individual totals for each tooth. Teeth with less wear scored fewer points and therefore the younger jaws had a lower numerical value.

The results of the analysis are shown in Table 74. Apart from one or two anomalies, the two methods were in broad agreement. The jaws aged over 72 months by Carter's method all had numerical values of over 40 using Grant's classification system. Jaws with values of 35 to 39 were found to lie between the ages of 36 to 60 months, and those with values of 30 to 34 were aged between 24 to 36 months. However, some stages of tooth wear in Grant's system appear to have lasted for a very long time. For example, Stage g of the M2 was found to be present in jaws ranging from 24 to 54-60 months in age, a very long time span in the animal's life. Similarly Stage g of the M1 and of the M3 also appear to have lasted for a long time (Table 74). Consequently jaws which had only one or two of the permanent molars present in these particular stages of wear could not be closely aged. Although further research is needed, it should be possible to correlate the two methods of analysis. One thing that has not been taken into consideration, however, is the possible variability in the rates of wear due to differential feeding which may limit the application of these techniques.

The tooth eruption data for the medieval period were obtained from a total of 271 mandibles and maxillae. These were divided up into samples dated to the eleventh to twelfth, thirteenth and fourteenth to fifteenth centuries. The earliest sample was further subdivided into samples dated to the eleventh to early twelfth centuries (Phase Md1) and the twelfth century (Md2) (Tables 72 and 73). The results continued to show the presence of a high percentage of young animals, especially in the early medieval period. The results indicated that over two-thirds of the animals had been killed by Stage 3 of their tooth eruption sequence and that over three-quarters were dead before Stage 5 was reached. The later medieval samples witness some decrease in this high rate of immature slaughter and the percentage of jaws which failed to reach Stage 3 fell to below 50%. The figures for Stage 5 also dropped by over 20% in comparison to the earlier medieval samples. The main peak of slaughter, as in the Roman period, occurred between Stages 2 to 3 of the tooth eruption sequence (15 to 26 months). In the sample from the thirteenth century deposits there was for the first time a notable concentration of jaws that belonged to animals that died between Stages 5 to 6 (approximately 42 to 60 months on Carter's ageing scale).

The fusion data gave consistent results throughout the medieval period (Table 75). The percentage of unfused proximal humeri and tibiae, and distal radii and femora (fusion age: 36 to 42 months) ranged between 69 to 82% in the samples involved. Close similarities were also found in the percentages of unfused proximal femora and ulnae (69 to 75%) and distal metatarsi epiphyses (52 to 60%). The percentage of unfused distal tibiae dropped from about 43% to about 32% between the twelfth and thirteenth

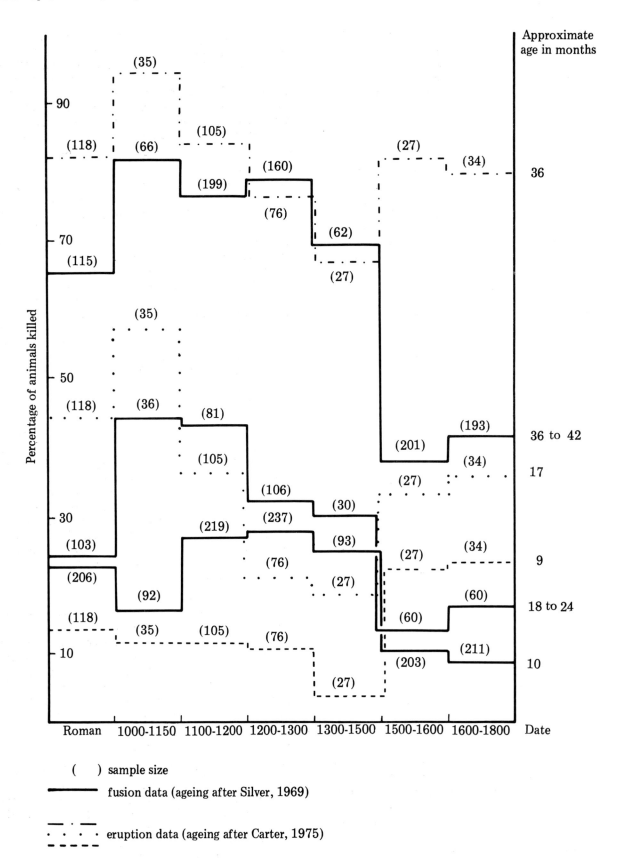

Figure 10   Sheep/goat ageing data.

century samples. This may reflect the fact that the period of peak slaughter began at a rather later age in the thirteenth century. The earliest epiphyseal fusion group (distal humerus, etc.) had percentages of unfused specimens that ranged from 16 to 28% of the samples, again suggesting that quite a high level of immature slaughter was taking place in the medieval town.

A comparison between the two sets of ageing evidence is made in Figure 10. This plots the cumulative percentages of sheep/goat killed against the age of the animals, using the estimates of Carter and Silver for the tooth eruption and fusion data respectively. In all the Roman and early medieval samples the fusion data produced slightly lower figures of animals killed by the age of 36 to 42 months than the maximum percentages obtained from the tooth eruption data for 36 months. Both sets of data do show a gradual trend throughout the medieval period towards a decrease in the slaughter of immature animals, although these continued to run at a very high rate. Both sets of evidence also indicate that a large proportion of animals brought to Exeter in this period were slaughtered between the ages of 18 and 36 months, if the ageing estimates are accurate and that a relatively large number of animals died during their first year.

The postmedieval period

A total of 61 jaws was studied; 27 were dated to the sixteenth century and 34 to the seventeenth and eighteenth centuries. The results from both these samples bore close resemblances to the results obtained from the thirteenth century sample (Tables 76-77), especially in the later stages of the eruption sequence. Once again, unfortunately, a significant number of the older jaws could not be aged with any accuracy, which accounts for the wide margins between the minimum and maximum percentage figures obtained in Table 76. The major change between these samples and that of the thirteenth century was the increased number of very young jaws. For the postmedieval period as a whole, 22.95% of the jaws had not reached Stage 1 of the tooth eruption sequence, compared to the figure of 10.53% attained from the thirteenth century sample. Other than these early mortalities, there were very few jaws that belonged to animals under two years of age. Certainly there was no peak of slaughter between Stages 2-3 as there had been in the earlier periods. It is interesting to note that as in the thirteenth century sample, a significant number of sheep was aged between 42 to 60 months, using Carter's ageing estimates (Table 77).

The fusion evidence (Table 78) was in direct contrast to the tooth eruption data. The results showed an appreciable drop in the number of unfused bones of all age groups. For the postmedieval period as a whole about 40% of the epiphyses with late fusion ages (the proximal humerus, etc.) belonged to immature animals, a decrease of over 35% in comparison with most of the medieval samples. The other fusion groups also revealed similar dramatic decreases in the number of unfused specimens. For example, only about 15% of the distal tibiae were unfused, compared with levels of 30 to 45% in the medieval samples. Similarly the youngest group of bones to fuse (the distal humerus, etc.) only had about 10% of the specimens in an unfused condition, a drop of over half compared with the equivalent medieval figures (Figure 10).

How, therefore, can two such conflicting sets of data be reconciled? To take the fusion data first, the samples from which the results were obtained were large ones, and, despite the variety in the richness of the postmedieval

deposits, the sample of sheep/goat appears not to have been influenced significantly by this factor. The fusion data from rich deposits such as GS F. 228 and TS F. 316 were similar to those of the much poorer Goldsmith Street deposits of the seventeenth and eighteenth centuries. The decrease in the proportion of the more fragile unfused bones cannot be ascribed to poorer preservation or hurried excavation; indeed the preservation of bone in the postmedieval features was better than in the earlier deposits.

One cannot, on the other hand, be as confident with the results obtained from the tooth eruption data. As was observed in Chapter 2, the proportion of jaw and skull fragments of sheep/goat fell to very low levels in many of the postmedieval deposits, and the sample of 61 jaws was much smaller than one would have expected in a sample of over 2,900 sheep/goat fragments. Secondly, there is good evidence that, due to a change in marketing practice, very few jaws of older animals were found in the deposits in question. For example, the fused distal radii (fusion age about 36 months) outnumbered the jaws of Stage 4 and above by a ratio of over 3:1 in the postmedieval samples. This was in contrast both to the medieval period, when the number of jaws was greater than the number of fused radii (1.31:1) and to the Roman period, when the numbers were roughly equal. Similar results were obtained from other epiphyses with late fusion ages.

Consequently, there seems to have been a change of marketing practice in the postmedieval period which resulted in considerably fewer skull and jaw fragments of the older sheep/goat population being associated with their major limb bones in the deposits investigated. Many of the animals must have been decapitated at slaughter and their skulls deposited elsewhere within, or outside, the city. This practice does not seem to have been carried out on the younger lambs to the same extent. Possibly they may more often have been roasted whole. Certainly in the deposits in question their skulls and jaws were much more frequently found with their limb bones.

As a result of this change in butchery practice, the postmedieval tooth eruption data cannot be directly compared with the earlier periods, since it seems likely that the number of older animals was significantly under-represented. Accordingly, the fusion data probably provide a more accurate indication of the slaughter pattern in this instance. There would therefore seem to have been a marked change in the rate of sheep/goat slaughter at Exeter in the postmedieval period, in that a much greater number of mature animals was killed.

DISCUSSION OF AGEING DATA

The interpretation of the ageing evidence depends to a large extent upon whether the tooth eruption and fusion ages as estimated by Carter (1975) and Silver (1969) are accurate when applied to the Exeter material. If one accepts that those ages approximate to the true age of the animals, there is evidence that the animals slaughtered for consumption in Exeter were not representative of the sheep/goat population in the area. Both sets of ageing data indicate a high rate of immature slaughter in the Roman and medieval periods. According to the tooth eruption data, 46 to 78% of the animals eaten in Exeter were younger than 25 months old in all the Roman phases and in the eleventh to thirteenth centuries. Animals culled before this age must have been bred principally for their meat value since, at most, they would have provided one fleece of wool only, as sheep yield their first fleece at about 18 months of age. The peak period of slaughter varied a little in the phases involved but most deaths occurred at between 15 to 30 months. One can therefore visualise a policy of the culling of the animals not required for breeding or other purposes at this age for their meat, the animals having already provided one, or perhaps two, fleeces of wool. To ensure the continuance of the stock, however, a certain number of ewes and rams would have to be kept alive for breeding purposes. Even if the remaining animals represented were all breeding stock, it is unlikely that they would have produced enough lambs to maintain such a high rate of immature slaughter, especially since the fertility rates of sheep were low by modern standards. In seventeenth century Norfolk, for example, this rate was only 0.5 to 0.8 lambs per ewe (Allison 1958: 103). In addition, the rate of natural deaths among lambs was also high in medieval times and losses of over 30% of the stock through disease have been recorded in several documentary records (Miller and Hatcher 1978:217). The same probably applied to the Roman period as well. The number of neonatal deaths and lambs that died during their first winter was comparatively low in the Exeter deposits and they are almost certainly under-represented. It is therefore probable that the Exeter samples do not contain a cross-section of the sheep population and that a considerable number of the breeding stock and the infant mortalities did not find a market in the town. It is possible to visualise a marketing system in which the majority of the stock not required for breeding or wool-growing purposes was culled with the view to satisfying the demands of the urban population for meat. The older animals and infant mortalities did not find a similar market in the town. In this respect it is unfortunate that as yet no rural sites in Devon can be compared to test this hypothesis.

Alternatively, the estimated ages of tooth eruption and fusion may both substantially underestimate the true age of the animals involved. Eighteenth century data for tooth eruption of 'semi-wild' hill sheep do show a much slower rate of dental development. According to this data, the premolars did not erupt prior to 30 months, while the M3 only erupted between three to four years (Silver 1969: 297). However, doubts have been raised about the validity of this data, since it allows a period of two years between the eruption of the M2 and M3, whereas the specimens from Exeter and other contemporary sites suggest a much shorter time span between the eruption of these two teeth. Despite these discrepancies, however, it is not impossible that the development of the Devon sheep was significantly slower than that allowed for above. If so, it is possible that the animals present in the Exeter deposits included a more representative cross-section of the sheep population, although young fatalities are still under-represented. In that case the overriding value of sheep was for their meat production with both wool and milk production taking only secondary roles.

It is interesting to compare both documentary and other archaeological evidence for sheep mortalities and exploitation patterns in these periods. The growth of a flourishing wool trade is frequently cited for some areas of southern Britain during the Roman period. The existence of this trade has been implied from Roman sources: Dionysius Perigates, for example, writing about 300 A.D., remarked upon the quality of British wool (Ryder 1964: 5). However, the ageing data from Exeter suggest that the southwest peninsula of Britain lay outside the area of this postulated wool trade, since the high rate of mortalities of young animals for meat in the city would suggest that wool was only a secondary product. A similar situation was found in the Portchester Castle Roman deposits. In a sample of 134 proximal humeri and tibiae and distal femora, 103 (76.87%) were found to be unfused and therefore, using Silver's ageing data, belonged to animals under 42 months in age (Grant 1975:394). The peak of slaughter was estimated to lie late in the second year of the animals' lives and the tooth eruption data produced results that bear close similarities to those of the Roman levels in Exeter. If a flourishing wool trade did develop in some areas of Roman Britain, the new economic trends did not supersede the necessity to obtain an adequate meat supply for the two centres in question.

The number of mature sheep represented in medieval Exeter was less than almost any other contemporary site investigated in southern and central England. This could be explained by regional variations in the exploitation of sheep or in a dichotomy between the ages of sheep eaten on rural and urban sites. There are arguments in favour of both these explanations from the piecemeal archaeological evidence available. In support of the latter explanation are the high percentages of adult animals represented on some rural medieval sites. At the medieval village of Upton, Gloucestershire, only 18% of the jaws found on the site had not reached Stage 4 of the tooth eruption sequence (all columns of M3 in wear) (Yealland and Higgs 1966:140). On the seven medieval sites investigated by Noddle (1975), the percentage of immature sheep represented in the medieval levels at North Elmham, Norfolk, was also low. This contrasted with the assemblages from two urban sites in Bristol, which had percentages of immature animals approaching the high levels from Exeter. The hypothesis of a rural-urban dichotomy is supported by some documentary evidence. In fifteenth century Norfolk the production of wool and store lambs was the principal motive in sheep breeding and Norwich's demand for mutton was satisfied by the sale of crones (old ewes) and pucks (poor quality lambs) drawn almost entirely from the surrounding district (Allison 1958:108). This implies that many of the wethers kept for the production of wool seem not to have found a market in the city to the same extent.

The division is not always clear-cut, however. The medieval deposits in the towns of Southampton and Kings Lynn contained higher percentages of mature individuals (Noddle 1975:255). The number of specimens from the former was very small, however, and may be misleading (Noddle 1974a: 336). The sample from Kings Lynn is larger (Noddle 1977) but the ageing data are presented differently from those of Exeter and the two sites cannot be closely compared. There is nevertheless a likelihood that there was regional variation in sheep exploitation related to the importance of producing surpluses of wool. Documentary evidence can again be used in support of this theory. Although it is accepted that the rearing of sheep for wool was the major pastoral occupation in the Middle Ages (Power 1941:21) and that the export of wool was by far the most important commodity in England's foreign trade (Lloyd 1977), not all regions enjoyed the boom to the same extent. It was the fine wools that were most in demand and those of the southwest were too coarse for the foreign market and were not exported (Power 1941:23). It was certainly less profitable for sheep farmers in Devon and Cornwall to concentrate on wool production because of the poor quality of the fleeces of their stock. An evaluation of 1343, which fixed a minimum price for wool, shows that the least expensive wool was grown in Cornwall and the second cheapest in Devon. The quality of Cornish wool was scornfully referred to as 'Cornish hair' (Trow-Smith 1957: 162). If the records of Tavistock Abbey can be taken to indicate the situation in the rest of Devon, the amount of wool obtained from each fleece was also lower than the national average. At Leigh, one of the abbot's manors, 156 fleeces sold in 1398 weighed an average of 1.08 lb. In the midlands and southern England on the other hand, the average weight of a short-woolled fleece ranged from 1.2 to 1.7 lb (Trow-Smith 1957:167). Accordingly, the southwestern farmers not only obtained very low prices for their wool but also produced less wool per fleece than most of the rest of England.

Therefore there was less incentive in terms of profit for large surpluses of wool to be produced in Devon in the medieval period. It would not be surprising to find that there was indeed a higher kill-off rate of immature animals for sale in market centres such as Exeter, which would have been more attractive economically for local sheep farmers than similar urban markets in areas of more profitable wool production. Devon does not seem to have been an important producer of wool in the twelfth and thirteenth centuries and it is of interest to note that on the Tavistock estates mature ewes were kept for their milking and breeding qualities rather than for their wool. Wool sales did not become more important until the middle of the fourteenth century (Finberg 1951:150). The increasing importance of Devon wool production in the later medieval period is also indicated by the appearance of large numbers of fulling mills during the thirteenth century (Carus-Wilson 1954:51). It is significant too that Exeter became one of the staple towns in the 1320s, through which the export of wool had to be directed (Lloyd 1977:115). This in itself merely confirms Exeter's importance as a commercial and trading centre at this period but it must also imply that the merchants in the city were now dealing with substantial quantities of wool, much of which must have been produced in Devon. Such an increase in the importance of wool production may also explain the relative increase of mature sheep represented in the Exeter deposits of the later medieval period, although the percentage of immature animals culled for meat remained predominant.

It is not until the postmedieval period that a dramatic change in the exploitation of sheep is evidenced and there is a substantial increase in the number of adult animals represented. If it is accepted that the estimated ages of tooth eruption and fusion approximate to the true age of the animals, the increase in the number of older animals shown by the fusion data may indicate that more of the breeding stock was now brought to the city along with the animals specifically reared for meat. In other words, the apparent change in the mortality rate may simply have been the result of a change in the marketing of animals. On the other hand, although the tooth eruption data overemphasises the importance of the younger animals in the postmedieval period, both sets of ageing evidence do suggest that very few animals were killed now between 15 to 30 months of age. Apart from lambs slaughtered in their first year, comparatively few of the stock brought to the city were under three years of age. It would seem, therefore, that most sheep eaten in Exeter were no longer reared especially for that purpose and slaughtered between 15 to 30 months, but instead were usually allowed to live to at least three years of age and often longer.

Similarly, even if the estimated ages of fusion and tooth eruption do substantially underestimate the actual ages of the animals, the evidence still indicates that many more animals were allowed to reach maturity in postmedieval times than previously. Consequently, there does seem to have been a change in the exploitation of sheep/goat in the postmedieval period, which cannot solely be explained by a change in marketing techniques. The reasons for this change may have lain in the increased importance of wool or dairy produce, both of which require a relatively high number of adult animals to provide annual supplies of fleeces and milk. The documentary evidence indicates that it was the former which was the prime factor in the new husbandry policy.

It was not until the fifteenth century that the wool obtained from Devon sheep, which was turned into broadcloths of coarse material called 'kerseys', became popular. It was the boom in this production that was the prime factor that brought such prosperity to Exeter in the fifteenth to seventeenth centuries. The demand for Devon kerseys began to snowball in the fifteenth century. The expensive cloths obtained from finer wool grown in other parts of England during the medieval period were now less popular and cheaper, coarser cloths were now in demand in Britain and in Europe. Export of Devon kerseys became common. In the 1440s more than 2,000 cloths per year were sent overseas. Despite a slump in the 1450s and 1460s, the export figures rose rapidly so that, in the years 1481 to 1483, an average of 6,000 cloths was exported. Thereafter exports averaged over 3,000 cloths a year for the rest of that century. The boom continued in the sixteenth century: between 1500 to 1510, for example, trade in Devon cloths averaged 8,600 cloths per year and the main industrial activity in Devon during that century was clothmaking (Carus-Wilson 1963:7-9; Thirsk 1967a:73). By the seventeenth century the demand for wool had outstripped the local supplies and Spanish wool which was imported to Exeter from the late fifteenth century, increased in quantity (Hoskins 1935:35). Westcote noted in 1630 (by which time serge manufacture had begun to increase in importance), that the large local wool supply which had previously been sufficient for the kersey industry was being supplemented by fleeces obtained from other southwestern counties, Gloucester, Worcester, Norwich, Wales, Ireland and London. Later in the seventeenth century wool was shipped to the Devon ports from Rye and Folkstone and increasing amounts were imported from Spain and Ireland (Stephens 1958:49).

Such a boom in the cloth industry undoubtedly encouraged the local flock owners to supply more wool. The demand increased the price of wool and it is therefore likely that the farmers would have kept more adult sheep in order to obtain their yearly growth of wool. The dramatic drop in the number of immature animals in the sixteenth century levels at Exeter, as evidenced by the epiphyseal fusion data, can most easily be explained by this phenomenon. Documentary evidence from England in general reveals that wethers were often finished for the butcher at four to five years of age in the sixteenth century (Thirsk 1967b:188). The same practice appears still to have been common in Devon at the end of the eighteenth century (Fraser 1794: 53). This would correlate with the concentration of jaws aged, using Carter's estimates, at between 42 to 60 months. Except for lambs killed at a few months old, meat production had become of secondary importance to that of wool.

Unfortunately, the Exeter deposits produced virtually no faunal material dated to the fifteenth century. Consequently the rise in the number of adult animals may have been more gradual than the evidence suggests. A bone sample from Plymouth investigated some years ago may cast light on the intervening period. Excavations on part of the medieval harbour in Woolster Street produced a quantity of animal

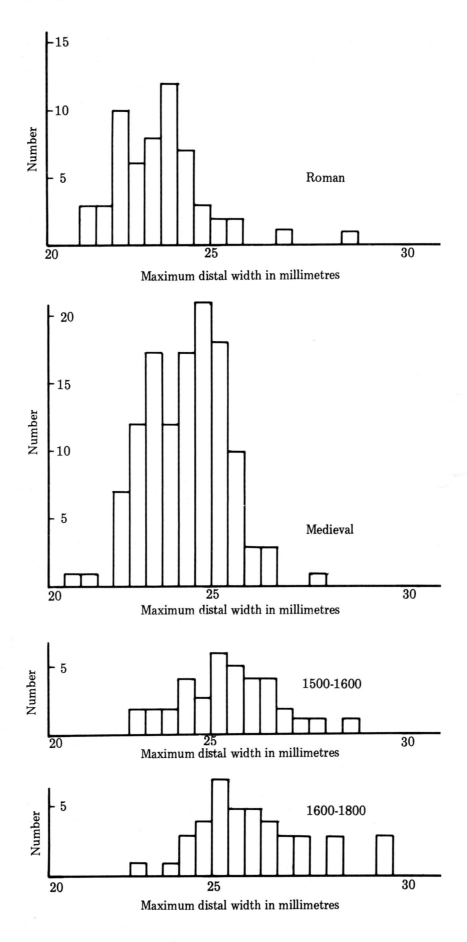

Figure 11   Histograms of sheep/goat tibiae measurements.

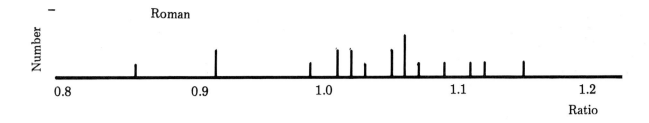

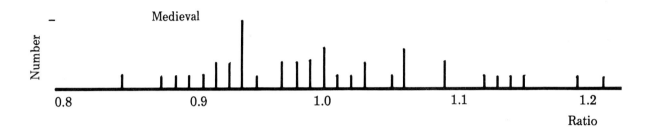

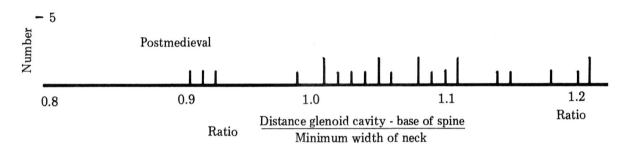

Figure 14   Metrical analysis of sheep/goat scapulae.

BUTCHERY PRACTICE

The skull and jaw

Skull and jaw fragments were found in the deposits commonly in the Roman and medieval periods. The brains of sheep/goat were probably a recognised food and therefore the skulls need not have been discarded at slaughter. Occasionally a deposit was found to contain a higher concentration of mandibles than average indicating the dumping of these waste bones, although this does not seem to have been done on a large scale in the deposits in question. In the postmedieval period the number of skulls and jaws found in the investigated deposits was much smaller, suggesting that many more of the skulls were discarded elsewhere and accordingly did not find themselves in domestic rubbish deposits. This practice does not seem to have applied to the younger animals for lamb skull and jaw fragments were still quite common. A fair proportion of the medieval and postmedieval skulls had been chopped in a cranial-caudal direction along the dorsal aspect of the skull to remove the brain.

The long bones

The vast majority of the major meat-bearing bones of sheep/goat were in a fragmentary condition. In the Roman period only 36 out of 1,105 (3.26%) fragments of humeri, radii, femora and tibiae were complete. In the medieval sample only 177 out of 2,670 (6.63%) of the bones were unbroken and finally in the postmedieval period 143 out of 1,307 (10.94%) long bones had both epiphyses intact. Of those bones the tibia was almost inevitably broken, as indeed were the humerus and femur, apart from a few isolated instances. The smaller radius tended to survive intact rather more frequently but was still predominantly fragmentary.

Many butchery marks were discovered on these bones. The most commonly found were those on the mid-shaft of the tibia. This was the case in all periods and nowadays, too, many leg joints of lamb are broken off at roughly the same point. Few proximal humeri have survived but the fairly common occurrence of severance near the distal articulation of these bones suggests that the scapula and most of the humerus were included in a single joint. The meat from the radius may have formed a separate joint, or more probably was used in stews. The distal shaft of the radius was another common butchery point where the feet of the animal were severed from the rest of the carcass. A greater concentration of complete femora and humeri was discovered in the postmedieval period, particularly in GS F.228 and TS F. 316. The lack of butchery on these bones, most of which belonged to mature animals is unusual. The phenomenon cannot be explained by the presence of several skeletons since very few of the skulls and metapodia were found associated with these bones.

Possibly the practice of boning out some of the limb joints was taking place at this time, or marrow extraction from these bones had become less important.

The metapodia

The smaller metapodia tended to show less fragmentation. In the Roman period 38 out of 292 specimens (13.01%) were complete. In the medieval period 157 out of 738 (21.27%) had both epiphyses present. The degree of fragmentation dropped noticeably in the postmedieval period in which 91 out of 260 specimens (35%) were unbroken. The metapodia have much less food value than the other long bones and may have been thrown away as waste, particularly in postmedieval times when, in certain cases, there was a scarcity of such bones in association with deposits that predominantly consisted of the major meat-bearing bones. In contrast, the seventeenth century deposits from the Valiant Soldier Inn site and several features on the GS I site, dated to the seventeenth and eighteenth centuries, had a marked concentration of such bones, indicating that they were treated differently from the other long bones.

The smaller metapodia would have required less butchery to be performed upon them and they may also have been boiled complete in many cases. The majority were in a fragmentary condition, however, and some butchery was undoubtedly practised upon them in all periods. These bones are ideal raw material for the manufacture of bone tools and ornaments. Indeed, the lack of fused distal metacarpi in the Roman period in particular may have resulted from the removal of the distal part of the bone for such manufacturing processes.

Vertebrae

As was the case with cattle, sheep/goat vertebrae were not sliced down their dorso-ventral axis before the postmedieval period, when the practice became widespread. Occasionally cutmarks were found on medieval specimens made when the vertebrae were cut laterally.

Conclusions

The butchery practised on sheep remained the same for a long period of time. It was only in the sixteenth century that a wholesale change in the methods of cutting up the carcass took place. No primary butchering area has as yet been found, although it seems clear that many fewer bones were discarded at slaughter compared with those of cattle. In the postmedieval period skull and jaw fragments were rarely found and to a lesser extent, metapodia fragments, suggesting that much more of the carcass was discarded at slaughter. The animals were cut into sides of mutton, a process which necessitated chopping the vertebrae dorso-ventrally, and their heads and feet were discarded. The butchery on the major limb bones seems to have changed little, however, although in some cases the leg bones may have been filleted out of these joints, perhaps by the butchers, or by individual cooks of rich households. This phenomenon was restricted mainly to the two richest deposits, which leads one to suspect that the practice may not have been widespread in the city.

SKELETAL ABNORMALITIES

The most common defect found in sheep/goat was that of periodontal disease. Many of the older jaws had teeth that were loose in their sockets and some also suffered from overcrowding. Both these deficiencies can be ascribed to poor planes of nutrition, a condition confirmed by the poor size of most of the stock. Six mandibles in the deposits had

no P2 present in an otherwise fully developed tooth row. This condition was also found in cattle and is not uncommon among deer and other ruminants as well. Degenerative conditions were very rarely discovered in sheep/goat bones, probably because in the Roman and medieval periods at least, most of the animals consumed in the city had not attained any great age. One sheep horn core showed severe restrictions in its growth, a condition possibly caused by an injury early in life. No sheep/goat bones bore any signs of trauma.

SUMMARY: THE EXPLOITATION OF SHEEP/GOAT

The horn/core evidence, other morphological criteria and the metrical analysis of certain bones all indicate that sheep greatly outnumbered goat in the sample. The archaeological evidence thus confirms the impression gained from documentary sources, in particular Domesday Book.

The ageing evidence is beset with difficulties and the interpretation of the results obtained from this analysis depends to some extent on whether the estimated ages for tooth eruption and fusion are accurate. If they are, then during the Roman and medieval periods a sizeable proportion of the flocks was raised simply to supply the city with meat, a fact indicated by the high mortality rate of immature individuals. The age of peak slaughter lay between 15 to 30 months, with a tendency in the later medieval period for this peak to be rather later than before. This may reflect the fact that wool production was becoming increasingly more important in the late Middle Ages, the older animals providing rather more wool. However, to maintain such a level of immature slaughter would require a much larger breeding herd than that evidenced in the deposits. If the estimated ages for sheep are accurate much of the breeding stock was not brought to the city for slaughter.

It is conceivable that many of the sheep and goats brought to the Exeter market were animals considered surplus to the requirements of the stock such as barren ewes and young males not needed for breeding or wool production.

During the postmedieval period the boom in the cloth trade as attested by the documentary evidence had a profound effect on sheep husbandry. Many more animals were allowed to reach full maturity in order to obtain as much wool off the animals as possible. Apart from the slaughter of some lambs, the pressure to obtain sufficient wool for the growing clothmaking industry precluded the slaughter of both ewes and wethers until they had provided several fleeces of wool. Mutton therefore became a more common item in the diet, as a result of a change not so much in dietary preferences as in market requirements.

The size of the stock was small even by contemporary standards and it was only in the postmedieval period that concerted efforts were made to improve the stock (which previously had consisted mostly of one type of animal) by the introduction of new breeds and by improved grazing and stocking policies. All the animals were probably herded to the city on the hoof in both Roman and medieval periods, and possibly in the postmedieval period as well. The butchery methods did change, however, in the sixteenth century, when carcases were cut into sides of meat for the first time. Some of these carcases may have been dressed and brought into the city by butchers not resident in the city, although most, no doubt, still passed through the hands of the resident butchers.

5.

THE EXPLOITATION OF PIG

AGEING DATA

As in the case of cattle, the tooth eruption sequence was divided into six stages and the evidence of both mandibles and maxillae was pooled in order to obtain a percentage of animals slaughtered before they had reached a particular stage in their dental development. The six stages chosen were:

Stage 1 p4 in wear.
Stage 2 Both columns of M1 in wear.
Stage 3 Both columns of M2 in wear.
Stage 4 P4 in wear.
Stage 5 The first column of M3 in wear.
Stage 6 All columns of M3 in wear.

The estimated ages for these stages of tooth development, as shown in Tables 80 to 82, are adapted from data derived from modern pigs (Silver 1969:298-9). Once again these ages may underestimate the true age of the animal. Improvements in breed and nutrition during the last 200 years may have accelerated tooth growth by as much as 50%, judging from some eighteenth century figures.

362 jaws were examined: 161 of Roman origin, 163 of medieval date and 38 of postmedieval date. The Roman sample was subdivided into three phases (55 to 100 A. D., 100 to 300, 300+) for this purpose. The three late first century burials of immature animals were excluded from the calculations, as it was considered that these were not killed for food and therefore were not typical of the overall slaughter pattern. The medieval sample was subdivided into specimens dated to the eleventh to twelfth, thirteenth, and fourteenth to fifteenth centuries. Both the postmedieval samples, dating to the sixteenth and seventeenth to eighteenth centuries respectively, were small.

The results from all periods showed a good deal of similarity. In all eight samples for which percentages were estimated, a minimum of over 40% of the jaws had not reached Stage 6. The number of immature deaths was in reality probably much higher since about 30% of the jaws were too fragmentary for this age determination to be made. Examination of the wear pattern of 22 jaws of twelfth century date, using Grant's system of wear pattern analysis (Grant 1975), suggested that seventeen of these had not reached Stage 6, only three had done so and the other two may just have reached that stage of development. Therefore, it seems likely that the actual numbers of stock slaughtered before their tooth eruption sequence was complete would have approached the maximum percentage figures given for Stage 6 of the sequence in Tables 80 to 82. This would indicate that over 80% of the pigs eaten in Exeter in all periods were killed before Stage 6 of the tooth eruption

sequence. The earlier stages in the sequence also reveal a high rate of immature mortalities. For example, the maximum percentage of animals killed before reaching Stage 4 ranged from 41 to 76% in the eight samples involved. The samples also showed some similarities for Stages 1 to 3 of the tooth eruption sequence.

The fusion data were divided into four groups of bones whose epiphyses fuse at approximately the same age. The sample was subdivided into the same groups as those employed for the tooth eruption evidence (Tables 83 to 85). In all periods, the latest group of epiphyses to fuse (proximal humerus, etc.), whose fusion ages in modern breeds range from 36 to 42 months (Silver 1969:285-6), revealed that over 85% of the epiphyses were unfused. In addition, the sample of epiphyses that fuse at about 24 months in modern breeds (the distal metacarpal and tibia and proximal first phalanx) contained large numbers of unfused specimens. Combining the data from each of these epiphyses, 58 to 64% of the Roman specimens were unfused and the equivalent percentages rose even higher in the subsequent periods ranging from 68 to 87% (Tables 83 to 85). These figures do not take into account the discrepancies between the various fusion points (for example, significantly more distal epiphyses of tibia were fused than distal metacarpals) but they do indicate the high rate of immature mortalities which took place throughout. The youngest group of epiphyses to fuse (the distal humerus, etc.) confirm this pattern. If these epiphyses fused within the first twelve months of the animal's life, as in more modern examples, the proportion of first year killings appears to have been higher in the Roman period (16 to 33% of the epiphyses were unfused) than in medieval times (9 to 18%). Nine of the 27 specimens (33.33%) of sixteenth century date were unfused. Once again differential preservation influenced the epiphyseal fusion data. Epiphyses with late fusion ages had less chance of survival than those with an earlier development. The figures, therefore, should not be taken literally, although the relative changes between periods can be monitored.

Both sets of ageing data therefore show that relatively few pigs reached maturity. Probably less than 10% of the pigs eaten were mature animals. This high rate of immature mortalities is to be expected, since, unlike cattle, sheep and goats, pigs have no economic importance other than their value for meat and skin. Accordingly, only a few breeding animals can be expected to reach maturity. The fecundity of the pig is great and the species can thus tolerate a very high rate of immature slaughter without endangering stock levels. The modern practice is to fatten up pigs for slaughter during their first year. Such an intensive exploitation was not matched in Roman and medieval

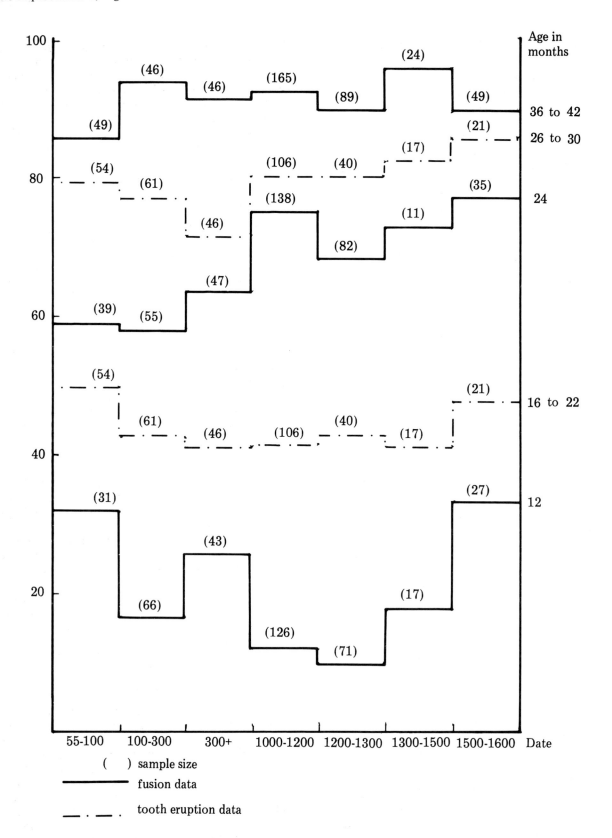

Figure 15   Pig ageing data.

Exeter, where a fair proportion of animals survived at least into their third year.

Despite the overall similarity between the mortality rates in the samples involved, there does seem to have been some variation in the peak killing periods of the pig. In the Roman period, to take the fusion evidence at its face value, there are indications that there was a fairly steady kill-off of pigs during the first three years. Taking the average percentage figures for the Roman period, about 25% of pigs were killed in their first year, about 35% in their second, and about 30% in their third. In the medieval period as a whole, however, the equivalent average percentage figures were about 13%, 59% and 20% respectively. There is therefore some evidence that the majority of the medieval stock was culled during their second year. This is confirmed by a closer analysis of the tooth eruption data. As can be seen from Figure 15, the permanent premolars (Stage 4) come into wear during the second year of the pig's life and Stage 5 is probably attained early in its third year (adapting Silver's estimates). In the medieval period, most of the animals seem to have been slaughtered between Stages 3 to 5 of the tooth eruption sequence. Of the 163 jaws examined, 28 (17.18%) were at a stage when the premolars were just coming into wear. Another 24 (14.72%) were killed between Stages 4 to 5. Using Grant's method of wear pattern analysis (Grant 1975), it was found that at least another fifteen mandibles (9.20%) belonged to animals killed between Stages 4 and 5. Consequently, at least 41.10% of the medieval pig jaws recovered belonged to animals slaughtered between the ages of about 16 and 26 months, mostly in the earlier part of that period.

There are only scant references to the breeding of pigs in the medieval period but it is interesting to note two examples Trow-Smith was able to cite. The first was gleaned from the accounts for the demesne farm at Stevenage, Hertfordshire, for 1273 to 1274. These revealed that pigs began to be fattened for the table at about eighteen months of age. At Wellingborough, Northamptonshire, it seems that pigs were slaughtered at almost any age in the fourteenth century but were not considered to make adult porkers or baconers until they were rising two years of age (Trow-Smith 1957:124-128). If a similar practice was carried out at Exeter, one would expect to see the peak of slaughter for animals aged between 18 to 24 months of age. The two sets of ageing data would seem to correlate broadly with this (Figure 15).

In the Roman period the majority of the stock was also killed between Stages 3 to 5 of the tooth eruption sequence, although the peak of slaughter was not so marked between Stages 4 and 5. There is some evidence that there was a greater number of animals killed in their first year, in particular demonstrated by the fusion evidence. This preference for younger animals may reflect the Roman liking for sucking-pig — a popular dish in Italy according to Roman authors (White 1970:318-320). It may be more than coincidence that the highest rate of immature deaths in the Roman period was in the first century, when the Roman influence in the garrisoned city was at its greatest. The level of young killings did not rise as high again until the sixteenth century (although this was a small sample and may not be reliable). It is interesting to note that the documentary evidence for the slaughter of pigs in the postmedieval period shows in certain areas of England that the age of slaughter generally decreased from that of the medieval period. In Leicestershire, for example, pigs were fattened in sties from the age of nine to twelve months (Thirsk 1967b:194). Similar advances in pig husbandry in

Devon at the same time would explain the increase in the number of animals killed in their first eighteen months, shown by the (admittedly limited) ageing data. It should be noted, however, that William Marshall observed that some pigs were not fattened for slaughter until they were two or three years of age in some parts of Devon at the end of the eighteenth century. He also noted that the 'native breed of the county' did not fatten up well until they were 18 to 24 months of age (Marshall 1796:256).

METRICAL ANALYSIS OF PIG

Humerus

The maximum width of the fused distal epiphyses of the humerus was plotted against its maximum thickness for specimens dated to the Roman and medieval periods (Figure 16). There was a greater concentration of medieval specimens in the smaller size range, perhaps indicating a decrease in stock size in the later period.

Radius

The proximal epiphysis of the radius fuses at approximately the same age as the distal humerus. Histograms of the maximum width of this epiphysis show a decrease in the average size of the bone between the Roman and medieval samples (Figure 17). In the Roman sample of 25 specimens the measurements were spread fairly evenly between 25.5 to 29.5 mm. In the medieval sample 27 out of the 51 specimens measured 24.5 to 26.5 mm.

The mandibular third molar

Enough measurements were obtained from the Roman sample to make comparisons of the length of the M3 with those of other sites. The length varied between 27.0 to 34.9 mm. When these measurements were compared with those obtained from the Roman sample from Fishbourne (Grant 1971:386), it was found that the pigs on the two sites displayed a similar range in size, with over 44% of the specimens in both cases lying in the 30.0 to 32.9 mm size range (Table 86). Using the same criteria, the pigs from the Saxon site of North Elmham were rather larger on average (Noddle 1975:256) than the stock on the Roman sites. Unfortunately, too few measurements were possible from the Exeter medieval and postmedieval samples for analysis to be worthwhile.

The overall size of the stock

Table 87 shows the range, mean, standard deviation and coefficient of variation of all pig measurements taken. Direct comparison between the results from the Roman and medieval periods would suggest superficially that the Roman stock was slightly larger. For example, the mean of the maximum distal width of the humerus in the Roman period was 37.4 mm, but only 35.7 mm in the sample of eleventh to twelfth century date. The mean of the maximum proximal width of the radius decreased from 27.1 to 25.9 mm, and the measurements of the distal scapula decreased to a similar degree. Unfortunately, because of the high mortality rate of immature animals, too few epiphyses with later fusion ages provided measurements for comparative purposes. It is interesting to note, however, that the measurements taken on the distal tibia, which fuses at about two years, did not show any significant change in size between the limited Roman and medieval samples. Too few bones of postmedieval date provided measurements to make realistic comparisons with the previous periods. One or two certainly belonged to larger animals, for example an astragalus of sixteenth century date measured 49.1 mm along its lateral length and a

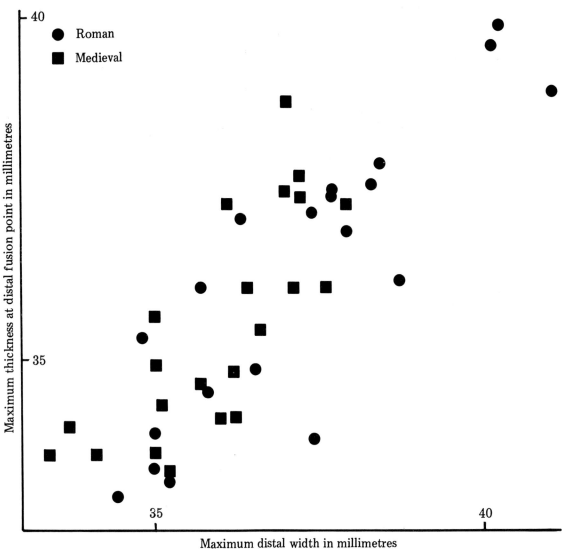

Figure 16   Scatter diagram of pig humeri measurements.

humerus of eighteenth century date possessed a maximum distal width of 47.1 mm. These were exceptional cases but it is certain that the postmedieval period saw great improvements in the size of the stock.

The results showed little evidence for the presence of wild boar, which is thought to have been a larger animal than domesticated pig. One Roman astragalus had a maximum length of 50.7 mm, which was over 10 mm larger than the second largest Roman example. The isolation of this specimen may indicate that it belonged to an animal of a different population, in which case the presence of wild boar could be postulated. Its rare occurrence would fit the pattern observed with regard to other game, which was also extremely rare in Exeter. On the other hand, of course, it is possible that the astragalus in question belonged to an exceptionally large domesticated pig.

BUTCHERY PRACTICE

The five burials uncovered all belonged to very young animals and showed no signs of butchering, being mostly too small to be of much food value. These were probably burials of diseased or casualty animals. Their presence may therefore indicate that some pigs were kept in the city itself.

The pig is an ideal animal for even small households to keep, being inexpensive to feed and maintain. In Worcester pigs were kept within the city even in the sixteenth century (Dyer 1973:207) and the same may have been the case in Exeter.

Apart from these burials, the pig samples revealed abundant evidence of butchery. Only 23 (5.23%) of the remaining 440 fragments of humeri, radii, femora and tibiae dated to the Roman period survived with both epiphyses intact. The pattern was similar in the later periods; 60 (8.02%) out of 748 medieval long bones were complete, and only 26 out of 250 (10.40%) specimens of postmedieval date were found to be unbroken. Such a high degree of fragmentation cannot be explained simply by damage during or after disposal and many of the breaks must have occurred during butchery. Much of the butchery on the long bones was similar to that of sheep/goat, which is to be expected, since the animals are of similar size and would require similar treatment of the carcass. Cut marks occurred on all types of long bone, the most common being knife cuts on the shaft of the humerus, a little above the distal epiphysis. Butchery marks associated with the disarticulation of the hind limb were also found quite frequently on the pelvis

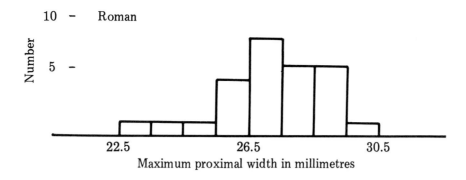

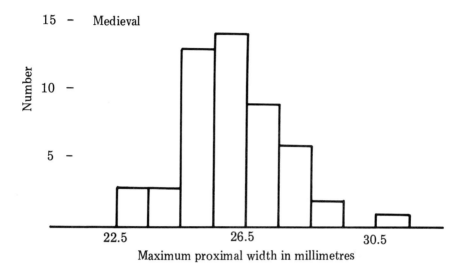

Figure 17   Histograms of pig radii measurements.

and proximal femur. Butchery on the smaller bones of young animals was less common and many more tended to be unfragmented because their smaller carcases required less butchery and marrow was not extracted from their bones.

In the Roman period, the MM/CC site produced a higher proportion of metapodials and phalanges (the bones from the trotters) than elsewhere. This was especially true in the third century deposits in which the numbers of these bones significantly biased the sample. Several features in particular had a marked concentration of the bones from pigs' trotters. None of the bones recovered bore evidence of butchery, although as pigs' feet are generally boiled after being cut off at the metapodials, there is no reason why these bones should bear cut marks. It cannot be said with certainty therefore whether these remains represent the refuse of a meal or the discarded trotters which were not considered as a source of food. The concentration of such bones in association with each other would suggest that the latter is the more likely alternative. Occasionally a similar concentration of such bones was found in later deposits, perhaps indicating a continuation in this butchery practice. The majority of the metapodials survived complete, being much smaller and less subject to butchery than cattle or sheep/goat metapodia.

As in the case of the other principal stock, the vertebrae of pig were rarely cut down the dorso-ventral axis to form chops until the sixteenth century, when it seems that the carcass was more often cut into sides of meat.

SKELETAL ABNORMALITIES

Apart from the young burials which may have belonged to diseased animals, although the cause of death was not manifest from the osteological evidence, most of the fragments showed no pathological conditions. Once again dental disease was the most common abnormality found, with some jaws displaying overcrowding and occasionally the crooked setting ot the cheek teeth. No signs of trauma were discovered on any of the bones.

SUMMARY: THE EXPLOITATION OF PIG

All, or virtually all, the pigs represented belonged to the domesticated variety. These were bred for their meat and lard, the only commodities for which they are economically important. This fact is reflected in the ageing data, which show a high number of immature deaths, a culling policy consistent with such a meat economy. The ageing evidence suggests that, apart from fluctuations in the number of first year deaths, the exploitation of pig gradually became more intensive during the periods of occupation at Exeter. The size of the stock showed no improvement until the post-medieval period. Like cattle and sheep/goat, many pigs would have been brought from outside the city for slaughter, although some pigs may have been kept by individual householders within the city itself.

6.

THE EXPLOITATION OF OTHER ANIMALS

A minimum of sixteen species provided the remainder of the mammalian sample. As was seen in Chapter 2, none of the animals discussed in this chapter was found in great numbers in the deposits. Only in a few isolated instances did they contribute more than 10% of the identifiable mammalian fragments in the phases involved. See page 65 for list of species discussed.

DEER

Red, fallow and roe deer contributed a total of 183 fragments in all the deposits. 78 of these, belonging to red and roe deer only, were discovered in the Roman levels (0.86% of the identifiable mammalian fragments). Red deer (43 fragments) was the slightly more common of the two, over half its fragments coming from the first century deposits. In the medieval period, deer became rarer still: just 42 fragments (0.25%) of the identifiable mammalian fragments belonged to the three cervid species present. Red deer (25 fragments) was still the most common; roe deer (nine fragments) continued to be recovered only in small numbers; fallow deer (eight fragments) was represented in the deposits for the first time in an early twelfth century context. No certain evidence of the latter species has been found among Roman or Saxon faunal remains and it may have been introduced by the Normans. No fallow deer fragments were found in the Roman levels at Exeter. Deer bones were also rarely found in the postmedieval deposits: only 62 deer fragments (0.85%) were discovered. 47 of these fragments were dated to Phase Pm1 (1500 to 1600), in which they contributed 1.22% of the identifiable mammalian fragments. The greater wealth indicated by the artifacts found in many features dated to this phase may also be reflected by the evidence of a more varied diet and a slight increase in the amount of venison eaten. Venison would presumably have been more expensive to buy than veal, mutton or pork which were available in much larger quantities at the time. Red deer (38 fragments) continued to be the species most frequently found in the postmedieval deposits. Fallow (fourteen fragments) and roe deer (ten fragments) completed the assemblage.

Other than the fact that few immature specimens were found, little can be said in detail of the intensity of exploitation of deer from the scanty ageing evidence. No red deer fragments from the Roman deposits belonged to young animals; a complete skull dated to the first century possessed fully erupted tooth rows and belonged to an adult animal. A fragment of a maxilla dated to the twelfth century did still have part of its deciduous tooth row present but this was the only example of an immature beast found in the medieval levels. A complete mandible of late eleventh century date belonged to a mature animal, and none of the

handful of bones which bore fusion evidence possessed unfused epiphyses.

Two immature roe deer were discovered in the Roman deposits; one mandible of military date did not have its third molar in wear and a distal epiphysis of a radius from a second century context was unfused. On the other hand, both the other mandibles discovered in this period had their tooth rows fully erupted. In addition, the two proximal humeri and the distal epiphysis of another radius were all fused, indicating that they belonged to adult animals. In the medieval sample, one metacarpus with an unfused distal epiphysis was the only example of a bone that definitely belonged to an immature animal. The only other fusion evidence consisted of two fused proximal epiphyses, of a radius and a tibia respectively. One maxilla fragment had its premolars in a state of wear that suggested that the jaw had belonged to a very old animal.

There was no evidence of immature animals among the few fragments of fallow deer discovered in the deposits.

No cut marks were discovered on any of the deer long bones but their fragmentary condition suggests that butchery did take place to obtain meat and marrow. In the Roman period, there were two instances of cut marks on red deer antlers. The first example, of late first century date, had several of its tines sawn off; the second, of fourth century date, revealed a chop mark close to the burr of the antler. Similar marks have been discovered on antlers recovered from other Romano-British sites, including the villa at Hemel Hempstead (Harcourt 1974b:260) and the fort at Longthorpe (Marples 1974:124). It is possible that the species was appreciated as much for the tool and ornament producing qualities of its antlers as for its meat — a fact supported by the high proportion of antler fragments found among the red deer assemblage at Exeter. There is a little documentary evidence for the exploitation of deer in the Exeter area. To the north of Exeter, the manor of Duryard belonged to the city from at least 1086, when it was mentioned in Domesday Book. The name means 'Deer-Park' and before deforestation the area would have provided an ideal habitat for such animals (Hoskins 1969:14). Despite this, it seems that venison played little part in the diet. This pattern is consistent with other medieval sites investigated. At Bristol, Hereford, Kings Lynn, Southampton (Noddle 1975:251), Kirkstall Abbey, Pontefract Abbey, Petergate (York) and Wharram Percy (Ryder 1961:106) the percentage of deer bone fragments was small in every case. In fact, of the Saxon and medieval sites investigated by Noddle, only Loughor Castle in southwest Wales produced a large percentage of deer bones (19%), presumably a result of the hunting practised by the almost completely as the tarsometatarsi of both sexes became larger. The same phenomenon can be seen in the postmedieval histograms of the other bones analysed. The greater variability in size resulted in a much greater overlap between male and female specimens resulting in the disappearance of the bimodal appearance of these histograms.

As yet, the above study has not taken into consideration the possibility that some of the bones belonged to capons (castrated males). Several tarsometatarsi in all periods possessed incomplete spurs but it was difficult to tell whether or not these spurs had simply been broken off close to their root. Nor is it established whether this genetic factor was present in capons in the periods in question. There is documentary evidence that caponising was practised by the sixteenth century and that capons were sold in the markets at Exeter (MacCaffrey 1958:81) and elsewhere in Devon by that time (Hoskins and Finberg 1952:263). There is documentary evidence that this practice was carried out in the medieval period, although how common this was is uncertain. The increase in the size of some of the fowl in the postmedieval period may have been due to innovations in poultry farming, such as selective breeding and the caponising of males for fattening and sale to the poultry markets. The improvement in size could also be the result of the introduction of superior breeds of fowl into the area during the sixteenth century.

Butchery marks were occasionally found on domestic fowl bones. The majority of limb bones were complete. Because of its small size, the fowl does not require much butchery. The leg and wing of chickens can be eaten without the necessity of cutting through any of the limb bones.

One ulna and one tarsometatarsus, both of medieval date, had suffered traumas, which had healed before the bird was killed and were not the cause of death.

The exploitation of the domestic fowl seems, therefore to have been quite intensive throughout the deposits, judging by the various strands of evidence discussed above. Besides providing meat, hens would have contributed eggs to the diet, although it is impossible to say exactly how important a commodity this would have been. Nowadays chickens lay about 200 eggs in their first year. They go off lay at the end of their first year and are then often killed. Hens brought back into lay in their second year produce fewer eggs. Whether hens were treated in a similar manner in Exeter is uncertain. Like pigs, poultry could have been kept by house-holders in the city and by most of the rural farmers, being inexpensive to keep and at the same time providing a cheap source of food. Poultry farming on a large scale probably did not take place until late in the postmedieval period. Certainly in the medieval period and before, there seems to have been little attempt at selective breeding or stock improvement.

Only three fragments of turkey were discovered in these excavations. The earliest of these was recovered in a context dated to the middle of the sixteenth century. This species was only introduced into Britain in the 1520s (Thirsk 1967a:194) and so its absence from previous deposits is to be expected. Even in postmedieval times, it seems that turkey was only a rare addition to the table.

No bones of peafowl were specifically identified, although some of the postmedieval domestic fowl bones reached peafowl proportions. Its absence is a little surprising since during the late sixteenth century it was mentioned alongside other poultry in the mayor's annual proclamation upon taking office (MacCaffrey 1958:81). However, like the turkey, it may only have been eaten on rare festive occasions, which would explain its absence from most domestic rubbish deposits.

Thirteen fragments of partridge were found, one of Roman origin, two belonging to the later medieval period, seven (from a minimum of two individuals) in GS F. 228 and three from TS F. 316. Its scarcity even in the latter opulent deposits indicates that this gamebird was not extensively exploited.

SWANS, GEESE AND DUCKS

The swan, like the turkey and peafowl, was probably only eaten on festive occasions. Its absence save for four fragments (from a minimum of two individuals) found in late thirteenth century contexts is therefore not surprising.

Greylag goose/domestic goose was the second most popular species of bird eaten in the city of Exeter. A total of 509 (12.01%) fragments from a minimum number of 92 (12.40%) individuals was recovered from the deposits investigated. However, only fifteen of these fragments were discovered in the Roman levels (Table 95). Despite the fact that the Romans are generally believed to have domesticated the greylag goose, it can only have played a minimal part in the diet at the time. It was not until the medieval period that the species became more important. The percentage of goose fragments varied between 14% and 29% in the nine medieval phases in which percentages were estimated. In each case it was the second most commonly found species, although it does not seem to have been reared as commonly around Exeter as in other areas of medieval Britain. During the sixteenth and seventeenth centuries, the goose may have become less popular. The percentage of fragments dropped to between 2% and 7% in the first three postmedieval phases. The seventeenth and eighteenth century sample (Phase Pm4) included seven fragments from one gosling, which accounts for the goose's unusually high percentage of 22.03% in the sample of 118 fragments.

A study of the minimum number of geese in all the phases showed a similar pattern to that of a simple count of fragments. In the larger Roman samples figures of 2 to 9% were obtained. The minimum numbers method employed on rather small samples tended to overestimate the importance of goose in these phases, since it was in fact only represented by a few fragments in each phase. During the medieval period, the percentage of goose obtained by this method ranged from 15 to 19% in the two largest samples. This figure dropped to between 6 to 10% in the larger postmedieval samples, a decrease paralleled by the count of fragments.

Although the numbers of geese on medieval sites would indicate that they were reared as poultry, their exploitation at Exeter was in marked contrast to that of domestic fowl. Only two out of a total of 172 limb bones were found to be unfused in the medieval sample. In the postmedieval deposits, apart from the partial skeleton of a gosling already mentioned, only four out of 39 long bones belonged to immature birds. It appears that the goose was much less intensively exploited than the domestic fowl. The birds were allowed to attain full size before they were fattened up for slaughter. The variation in the size of goose was less than in fowl. Only the carpometacarpus and tarsometatarsus produced samples large enough for measurements to be analysed. These had a coefficient of variation of 4 to 6. There was no significant change in the mean size of these bones between the medieval and post-medieval periods (Table 100). A greater percentage of geese bones were broken than those of domestic fowl. This is to be expected, since the goose is a much larger bird and the wings and legs would have to be broken up to allow manageable servings to be provided.

The mallard or its domesticated form was the commonest duck species found at Exeter, although it played only a small part in the diet. 142 (3.35%) fragments from a minimum of 41 (5.53%) individuals were recovered. Only eighteen of these fragments were of Roman date. The duck's scarcity continued throughout the medieval period. With the exception of one small sample dated to the late thirteenth and early fourteenth centuries, none of the medieval phases produced percentages of duck of over 2.25% of the avian fragments. In most of them the figure was below 1%. The percentage obtained by the minimum numbers method were rather higher, although once again the presence of a few fragments in each phase overvalued the importance of this and other rare species in the sample. The mallard is known to have been domesticated in medieval times and it is possible that it was also reared as poultry during the Roman period (Eastham 1971:391). However, the paucity of its remains in Exeter indicated that it was either kept in captivity in small numbers, or simply hunted occasionally as game. In the Roman levels of Portchester and Fishbourne (Eastham 1971, 1975) bones of the mallard species ranked second only to domestic fowl and ahead of goose. In Exeter, eighteen fragments of duck were found in comparison to fifteen of goose, indicating that neither was an important component in the diet of the townsfolk.

The sixteenth century deposits accounted for over half the fragments of duck found in the deposits. Two pits accounted for all but five of the 86 bones recovered; 58 fragments were discovered in GS F. 228, while 23 came from GS F. 291. The latter deposit was interesting in that all the bones belonged to the wings. It is probable that these were the discarded refuse from meals or a feast since a lot of meat can be extracted from these bones. In GS F. 228 both the wing and leg bones of duck were represented in roughly equal numbers. The amount of duck in these two features was exceptional and produced a percentage of that species in the sixteenth century phase of 8.11% of the bird bone fragments and 10.53% of the minimum number of individuals represented. In the rest of the postmedieval phases, the number of duck bones was no higher than their previous low levels.

Only two bones in the whole of the deposits, one of Roman origin and one from GS F. 228, belonged to immature birds. Their mortality rate was therefore similar to goose, and indeed to most gamebirds in this respect. Too few measurements were taken for any conclusions to be made about the overall size of the ducks. Except in the rich deposits of the late sixteenth century, they appear to have been of very little importance in the economy.

Other goose and duck species were very rare indeed. One bone of a small goose species was discovered, possibly belonging to the white-fronted species (*Anser albifrons*). Of the smaller duck species, only teal (eleven fragments) and wigeon (three fragments) were identified. Seven of the teal bones came from the sixteenth century phase and indicate that this bird was a source of game in that period at least. The teal nowadays breeds quite commonly in the area, and the wigeon is a common winter visitor. Both birds are edible but wild duck and geese do not seem to have been caught in large numbers.

WADERS

A total of eleven wading species (other than swans, ducks and geese) was identified. By far the most common of these was the woodcock. A total of 169 (3.99%) fragments from a minimum of 52 (7.55%) individuals was found. In the deposits as a whole, therefore, the woodcock ranked third behind domestic fowl and goose. The species was found relatively more commonly in the Roman and early medieval levels than later. It was reasonably popular throughout the Roman phases, contributing approximately 10% of the avian fragments in the samples from the third and fourth centuries. In the earlier medieval phases, the species provided between 5 and 10% of the number of bird bone fragments. In the later medieval and postmedieval periods the level of woodcock declined usually to under 5% of the total avian sample. It was still, however, the most commonly found gamebird in the deposits.

This decline is not so marked in the results obtained from the minimum numbers method, although the same general trend can be observed (Tables 95-97). In modern times, the woodcock is found commonly as a non-breeding winter visitor in Devon and Cornwall, although it still breeds in Dorset and Wales (Heinzel *et al.* 1972:328). There is good documentary evidence to suggest that it was a winter visitor in the sixteenth century as well. Richard Carew, writing about the fauna of his native Cornwall, said:

'But amongst all the rest (wild birds) the inhabitants are most behoven to woodcock, who (when the seasons of the year affordeth)
flock to them in great abundance.' (Halliday 1953:108). Woodcock was constantly in demand between October and February in the sixteenth century at Tavistock Abbey. It was not recorded in the other months (Hoskins and Finberg 1952:263). The species was therefore regarded principally as a winter food resource, at the season when it was common in the region.

The woodcock's more common occurrence in the Roman and early medieval periods may be due in part to the fact that it was present in the area all the year round. There is some documentary evidence to show that prior to the early medieval period, when the land around Exeter was drained by the cutting of leats, the area around the river Exe below the city was marshland (Hoskins 1969:24). The decline in the number of woodcock around Exeter from this time could reflect a decrease in the amount of marshland in the area, which either compelled the species to stop breeding in the area, or attracted fewer winter migrants. Alternatively the decline in the relative number of woodcock may simply be a reflection of the fact that more domesticated poultry was kept and consumed by the inhabitants of Exeter.

The hypothesis that some degree of environmental change has taken place in the countryside in the vicinity of Exeter during the past 2,000 years would also help to explain the presence of the common crane in a late first century context. This species is not now found in the British Isles but is known to have bred on areas of extensive marsh such as the Fens in historic times. Its bones have been recorded on several sites including that of medieval Southampton (Bramwell 1975:340). The crane was the largest species of bird found at Exeter and of undoubted food value.

Of the remaining wading species, all except the two plover species and the green sandpiper attain a length of at least

Species		GS No	GS %	TS No	TS %	MM/CC No	MM/CC %
Cattle	F	245	29.91	102	47.01	126	27.16
	M	12	16.67	11	35.48	13	27.08
Sheep/Goat	F	311	37.97	68	31.34	169	36.42
	M	33	45.83	11	35.48	13	27.08
Pig	F	236	28.82	41	18.89	148	31.90
	M	21	29.17	5	16.13	12	25.00
Red Deer	F	–	–	4	1.84	1	0.22
	M	–	–	2	6.45	1	2.08
Roe Deer	F	1	0.12	1	0.46	1	0.22
	M	1	1.39	1	3.23	1	2.08
Hare	F	13	1.59	–	–	3	0.65
	M	2	2.78	–	–	1	2.08
Horse	F	5	0.61	–	–	14	3.02
	M	1	1.39	–	–	5	10.42
Dog	F	7	0.86	1	0.46	2	0.43
	M	1	1.39	1	3.23	2	4.17
Cat	F	1	0.12	–	–	–	–
	M	1	1.39	–	–	–	–
TOTAL MAMMAL	F	819	100	217	100	464	100
	M	72	100	31	100	48	100
Bird	F	57	6.47	11	4.83	18	3.73
	M	19		4		8	
Fish	F	5	0.57	–	–	1	0.21
TOTAL FRAGMENTS		881	100	228	100	483	100
TOTAL UNIDENTIFIED		1039		130		214	

TABLE   3   (i)

*Number of fragments and minimum number of individuals
represented in phase R5 (A.D.100 - A.D.200)*

F = number of fragments identified.

M = minimum number of individuals represented.

Species		RS No	HS No	HL No	BS No	TOTAL R5 No	%
Cattle	F	31	55	57	89	705	38.63
	M	7	4	3	7	57	28.79
Sheep/Goat	F	24	20	9	14	615	33.70
	M	4	4	3	4	72	36.36
Pig	F	5	11	3	4	448	24.55
	M	2	3	2	1	46	23.23
Red Deer	F	–	–	–	–	5	0.27
	M	–	–	–	–	3	1.52
Roe Deer	F	1	–	–	–	4	0.22
	M	1	–	–	–	4	2.02
Hare	F	–	–	–	–	16	0.88
	M	–	–	–	–	3	1.52
Horse	F	–	–	–	1	20	1.10
	M	–	–	–	1	7	3.54
Dog	F	–	1	–	–	11	0.60
	M	–	1	–	–	5	2.53
Cat	F	–	–	–	–	1	0.05
	M	–	–	–	–	1	0.51
TOTAL	F	61	87	69	108	1825	100
MAMMAL	M	14	12	8	13	198	100
Bird	F	2	2	–	1	91	4.74
	M	1	1	–	1	34	
Fish	F	–	–	–	–	6	0.31
TOTAL FRAGMENTS		63	89	69	109	1922	100
TOTAL UNIDENTIFIED		45	70	79	111	1688	

TABLE   3   (ii)

Number of fragments and minimum number of individuals represented in phase R5 (A.D.100 - A.D.200)

F = number of fragments identified.

M = minimum number of individuals represented.

		TS	MM/CC		RS	HL	BS	HS	TOTAL R6	
Species		No	No	%	No	No	No	No	No	%
Cattle	F	35	163	33.20	25	3	5	4	235	35.29
	M	5	12	29.27	2	1	1	1	22	31.88
Sheep/Goat	F	37	107	21.79	8	–	–	–	152	22.82
	M	6	8	19.51	2	–	–	–	16	23.19
Pig	F	33	143	29.12	3	1	–	–	180	27.03
	M	4	13	31.70	1	1	–	–	19	27.54
Red Deer	F	1	2	0.41	–	–	–	–	3	0.45
	M	1	1	2.44	–	–	–	–	2	2.90
Roe Deer	F	–	3	0.61	–	–	–	–	3	0.45
	M	–	1	2.44	–	–	–	–	1	1.45
Hare	F	19*	7	1.43	–	–	–	–	26	3.90
	M	2	2	4.88	–	–	–	–	4	5.80
Dog	F	–	23*	4.68	1	–	–	–	24	3.60
	M	–	2	4.88	1	–	–	–	3	4.35
Cat	F	–	1	0.20	–	–	–	–	1	0.15
	M	–	1	2.44	–	–	–	–	1	1.45
Badger	F	–	42*	8.55	–	–	–	–	42	6.31
	M	–	1	2.44	–	–	–	–	1	1.45
TOTAL	F	125	491	100	37	4	5	4	666	100
MAMMAL	M	18	41	100	6	2	1	1	69	100
Bird	F	28	32	6.08	2	1	–	–	63	8.55
	M	11	13		1	1	–	–	26	
Fish	F	5	3	0.57	–	–	–	–	8	1.09
TOTAL FRAGMENTS		158	526	100	39	5	5	4	737	100
TOTAL UNIDENTIFIED		151	348		52	3	2	–	556	

TABLE 4

Number of fragments and minimum number of individuals represented in phase R6 (A.D.200 - A.D.300)

F = number of fragments identified.

M = minimum number of individuals represented.

* Badger includes 42 fragments from one burial.
  Dog includes 22 fragments from one burial.
  Hare includes 15 fragments from one burial.

Species		GS No	GS %	TS No	TS %	MM/CC No	MM/CC %	RS No	TOTAL R8 No	TOTAL R8 %
Cattle	F	808	52.00	589	69.54	140	47.78	66	1603	56.94
	M	17	24.29	22	40.74	7	25.00	4	50	30.68
Sheep/Goat	F	375	24.13	97	11.45	43	14.68	33	548	19.47
	M	22	31.43	14	25.93	7	25.00	4	47	28.83
Pig	F	290	18.66	138	16.29	85	29.01	21	534	18.97
	M	15	21.43	11	20.37	6	21.42	2	34	20.86
Red Deer	F	7	0.45	-	-	1	0.34	-	8	0.28
	M	3	4.29	-	-	1	3.57	-	4	2.45
Roe Deer	F	6	0.39	-	-	-	-	-	6	0.21
	M	1	1.43	-	-	-	-	-	1	0.61
Hare	F	7	0.45	1	0.12	3	1.02	1	12	0.43
	M	3	4.29	1	1.85	1	3.57	1	6	3.68
Horse	F	14	0.90	17	2.01	8	2.73	-	39	1.39
	M	3	4.29	3	5.56	2	7.14	-	8	4.91
Dog	F	13	0.84	4	0.47	12	4.10	-	29	1.03
	M	2	2.86	2	3.70	3	10.71	-	7	4.29
Cat	F	10	0.64	1	0.12	-	-	-	11	0.39
	M	2	2.86	1	1.85	-	-	-	3	1.84
Fox	F	4	0.26	-	-	-	-	-	4	0.14
	M	1	1.43	-	-	-	-	-	1	0.61
Hedgehog	F	-	-	-	-	1	0.34	-	1	0.04
	M	-	-	-	-	1	3.57	-	1	0.61
Woodmouse	F	20*	1.29	-	-	-	-	-	20	0.71
	M	1	1.43	-	-	-	-	-	1	0.61
TOTAL	F	1554	100	847	100	293	100	121	2815	100
MAMMAL	M	70	100	54	100	28	100	11	163	100
Bird	F	141	8.16	45	5.04	23	7.26	6	215	7.00
	M	26		11		8		2	47	
Fish	F	33	1.91	1	0.11	1	0.32	6	41	1.34
TOTAL FRAGMENTS		1728	100	893	100	317	100	133	3071	100
TOTAL UNIDENTIFIED		1812		556		188		167	2723	

TABLE 5

Number of fragments and minimum number of individuals represented in phase R8 (A.D.300+)

F = number of fragments identified.

M = minimum number of individuals represented.

* Woodmouse includes 20 fragments from one burial.

Pig	M	% Stock	M.R.B.	S.M.	Cat.1	Cat.2	Cat.3	Cat.4	Cat.5	Cat.6	Cat.7	Chi^2
GS-R1	7	25.00	m.	57	0.39	0.25	0.14	0.11	0.05	0.07	0.00	A
TS-R1	4	22.22	ca.	29	-	-	-	-	-	-	-	-
MM/CC-R1	8	40.00	mx.	49	0.37	0.29	0.08	0.06	0.08	0.06	0.06	A
GS-R2	10	37.04	sc.	50	0.28	0.38	0.18	0.06	0.02	0.00	0.08	A
MM/CC-R2	8	33.33	m.	65	0.28	0.20	0.17	0.11	0.08	0.09	0.08	A
GS-R5	21	31.82	m.	150	0.37	0.29	0.13	0.09	0.05	0.01	0.05	A
TS-R5	5	18.52	m.	36	-	-	-	-	-	-	-	-
MM/CC-R5	12	31.58	h.	100	0.22	0.29	0.20	0.12	0.05	0.09	0.03	A
MM/CC-R6	13	39.39	pl.	108	0.20	0.22	0.14	0.21	0.06	0.16	0.00	**
GS-R8	9	26.47	t.te.	98	0.29	0.26	0.20	0.10	0.08	0.03	0.04	A
TS-R8	11	23.40	m.	101	0.26	0.27	0.24	0.15	0.03	0.03	0.03	A
MM-R8	4	36.36	u.pl.	39	-	-	-	-	-	-	-	-
CC-R8	2	22.22	h.r.f.	15	-	-	-	-	-	-	-	-
RS-R8	2	20.00	te.	12	-	-	-	-	-	-	-	-
TOTAL	116	29.59	-	909	0.29	0.27	0.17	0.12	0.05	0.06	0.04	

TABLE 9 (ii)
Minimum number of individuals and category proportions
of the principal stock animals - Roman phases
(excluding RS F.363, GS F.49, F.60, L.424, F.47, F.160, F.618)

M = minimum number of individuals
M.R.B. = most represented bone(s).
S.M. = sum of minimum numbers.
*** = sample significantly different at 1% level of chi-squared.*
A = sample within 5% level of chi-squared.
m = mandible; te = teeth; sk = skull; mx = maxilla; sc = scapula;
h = humerus; f= femur; r = radius; u = ulna; t = tibia;
mc = metacarpus; pl = first phalanx; p2 = second phalanx;
ca = calcaneum.

		GS, TS, MM/CC - R1				GS - R2	
Species	M	Min.Wt.	% meat	M	Min.Wt.	% meat
Cattle	19	9,500 lb.	72.63	6	3,000 lb.	64.38
Sheep/Goat	28	1,680 lb.	12.84	11	660 lb.	14.16
Pig	19	1,900 lb.	14.53	10	1,000 lb.	21.46

		TS - R5				GS - R8	
Species	M	Min.Wt.	% meat	M	Min.Wt.	% meat
Cattle	11	5,500 lb.	82.58	10	5,000 lb.	73.53
Sheep/Goat	11	660 lb.	9.91	15	900 lb.	13.24
Pig	5	500 lb.	7.51	9	900 lb.	13.24

		TS - R8				MM/CC, RS - R8	
Species	M	Min.Wt.	% meat	M	Min.Wt.	% meat
Cattle	22	11,000 lb.	85.01	11	5,500 lb.	79.02
Sheep/Goat	14	840 lb.	6.49	11	660 lb.	9.48
Pig	11	1,100 lb.	8.50	8	800 lb.	11.49

TABLE 10

Estimations of minimum meat weights of the principal stock animals in statistically similar Roman deposits

M = minimum number of individuals represented.
Min.Wt. = minimum amount of meat represented.
Meat weight of a cow estimated to be 500 lb.
Meat weight of a sheep estimated to be 60 lb.
Meat weight of a pig estimated to be 100 lb.

Species		GS I-II No	GS I-II %	GS III No	GS III %	TS No	TS %	TOTAL Md3 No	TOTAL Md3 %
Cattle	F	160	30.89	180	27.15	93	33.70	433	29.72
	M	8	20.51	12	27.27	8	32.00	28	25.93
Sheep/Goat	F	279	53.86	300	45.25	102	36.96	681	46.74
	M	18	46.15	15	34.09	8	32.00	41	37.96
Pig	F	63	12.16	105	15.84	41	14.86	209	14.34
	M	5	12.82	7	15.91	4	16.00	16	14.81
Red Deer	F	4	0.77	-	-	1	0.36	5	0.34
	M	2	5.13	-	-	1	4.00	3	2.78
Fallow Deer	F	-	-	1	0.15	--	-	1	0.07
	M	-	-	1	2.27	-	-	1	0.93
Roe Deer	F	1	0.19	-	-	-	-	1	0.07
	M	1	2.56	-	-	-	-	1	0.93
Hare	F	1	0.19	2	0.30	1	0.36	4	0.28
	M	1	2.56	2	4.55	1	4.00	4	3.70
Rabbit	F	-	-	5	0.75	-	-	5	0.34
	M	-	-	1	2.27	-	-	1	0.93
Horse	F	3	0.58	1	0.15	2	0.72	6	0.41
	M	1	2.56	1	2.27	1	4.00	3	2.78
Dog	F	-	-	7*	1.06	-	-	7	0.48
	M	-	-	1	2.27	-	-	1	0.93
Cat	F	6	1.16	61	9.20	36*	13.04	103	7.07
	M	2	5.13	3	6.82	2	8.00	7	6.48
Rat	F	1	0.19	-	-	-	-	1	0.07
	M	1	2.56	-	-	-	-	1	0.93
Rodent sp.	F	-	-	1	0.15	-	-	1	0.07
	M	-	-	1	2.27	-	-	1	0.93
TOTAL MAMMAL	F	518	100	663	100	276	100	1457	100
	M	39	100	44	100	25	100	108	100
Bird	F	53	8.37	75	8.58	20	5.53	148	7.92
	M	10		9		8		27	
Fish	F	62	9.79	136	15.56	66	18.23	264	14.13
TOTAL FRAGMENTS		633	100	874	100	362	100	1869	100
TOTAL UNIDENTIFIED		793		663		253		1709	

TABLE 17

Number of fragments and minimum number of individuals represented in phase Md3 (A.D.1000 - A.D.1200)

F = number of fragments identified.

M = minimum number of individuals represented.

* Dog includes 7 fragments from one burial.
  Cat includes 35 fragments from one burial.

Cattle	F	% Stock	Cat.1	Cat.2	Cat.3	Cat.4	Cat.5	Cat.6	Cat.7	Chi^2
GS I-II	160	31.87	0.26	0.30	0.25	0.11	0.03	0.02	0.04	A
GS III	180	30.77	0.31	0.28	0.20	0.07	0.07	0.07	0.01	A
TS	93	39.41	0.22	0.28	0.27	0.10	0.10	0.01	0.03	A
TOTAL	433	32.73	0.27	0.29	0.23	0.09	0.06	0.03	0.03	

Sheep/Goat	F	% Stock	Cat.1	Cat.2	Cat.3	Cat.4	Cat.5	Cat.6	Cat.7	Chi^2
GS I-II	279	55.58	0.27	0.29	0.28	0.12	0.03	0.01	0.00	A
GS III	300	51.28	0.25	0.34	0.24	0.12	0.01	0.04	0.01	A
TS	102	43.22	0.25	0.35	0.23	0.11	0.01	0.02	0.02	A
TOTAL	681	51.47	0.26	0.32	0.25	0.12	0.02	0.03	0.01	

Pig	F	% Stock	Cat.1	Cat.2	Cat.3	Cat.4	Cat.5	Cat.6	Cat.7	Chi^2
GS I-II	63	12.55	0.52	0.17	0.13	0.11	0.03	0.03	0.00	**
GS III	105	17.95	0.19	0.21	0.21	0.28	0.03	0.06	0.02	A
TS	41	17.37	0.29	0.27	0.27	0.12	0.02	0.00	0.03	A
TOTAL	209	15.80	0.31	0.21	0.20	0.20	0.03	0.04	0.01	

TABLE 18

*Number of fragments and category proportions of the
principal stock animals - phase Md3*

F = number of fragments identified.

*** = sample significantly different at the level of chi-squared.*

A = sample within 5% level of chi-squared.

116

Cattle	M	% Stock	M.R.B.	S.M.	Cat.1	Cat.2	Cat.3	Cat.4	Cat.5	Cat.6	Cat.7	Chi^2
GS I-II	8	25.81	te.	77	0.22	0.29	0.18	0.14	0.05	0.04	0.08	A
GS III	12	35.29	sk.	90	0.27	0.26	0.19	0.08	0.11	0.07	0.02	A
TS	8	40.00	r.	63	0.17	0.29	0.25	0.08	0.14	0.02	0.05	A
TOTAL	28	29.41	-	230	0.23	0.27	0.20	0.10	0.10	0.05	0.05	

Sheep/Goat	M	% Stock	M.R.B.	S.M.	Cat.1	Cat.2	Cat.3	Cat.4	Cat.5	Cat.6	Cat.7	Chi^2
GS I-II	18	58.07	t.	145	0.22	0.32	0.29	0.10	0.04	0.02	0.01	A
GS III	15	44.12	r.	138	0.21	0.31	0.22	0.15	0.02	0.06	0.03	A
TS	8	40.00	sk.f.t.	71	0.23	0.31	0.27	0.13	0.01	0.03	0.02	A
TOTAL	41	48.24	-	354	0.22	0.31	0.26	0.13	0.03	0.04	0.02	

Pig	M	% Stock	M.R.B.	S.M.	Cat.1	Cat.2	Cat.3	Cat.4	Cat.5	Cat.6	Cat.7	Chi^2
GS I-II	5	16.13	m.	42	0.36	0.24	0.17	0.14	0.05	0.05	0.00	A
GS III	7	20.59	t.	68	0.22	0.19	0.21	0.25	0.04	0.06	0.03	A
TS	4	20.00	r.t.	33	-	-	-	-	-	-	-	-
TOTAL	16	18.82	-	143	0.27	0.23	0.21	0.17	0.04	0.04	0.02	

TABLE 19

*Minimum number of individuals and category proportions
of the principal stock animals - phase Md3*

M = minimum number of individuals
M.R.B. = most represented bone(s).
S.M. = sum of minimum numbers.
A = sample within 5% level of chi-squared.
te = teeth; sk = skull; m = mandible; r = radius;
f = femur; t = tibia.

Species		GS I-II No	GS III No	%	TS No	TOTAL Md4 No	%
Cattle	F	24	83	36.40	7	114	34.76
	M	3	5	26.32	2	1o	25.00
Sheep/Goat	F	37	71	31.14	16	124	37.80
	M	5	6	31.58	5	16	40.00
Pig	F	8	46	20.18	5	59	17.99
	M	2	3	15.79	1	6	15.00
Red Deer	F	–	2	0.88	–	2	0.61
	M	–	1	5.26	–	1	2.50
Hare	F	1	–	–	–	1	0.3
	M	1	–	–	–	1	2.50
Horse	F	2	2	0.88	–	4	1.22
	M	2	1	5.26	–	3	7.50
Cat	F	–	23*	10.09	–	23	7.01
	M	–	2	10.53	–	2	5.00
Rat	F	–	1	0.44	–	1	0.30
	M	–	1	5.26	–	1	2.50
TOTAL MAMMAL	F	72	228	100	28	328	100
	M	13	19	100	8	40	100
Bird	F	9	39	13.22	3	51	12.29
	M	3	9		2	14	
Fish	F	6	28	9.49	2	36	8.6
TOTAL FRAGMENTS		87	295	100	33	415	100
TOTAL UNIDENTIFIED		82	349		43	474	

TABLE 20

Number of fragments and minimum number of individuals represented in phase Md4 (A.D.1150 - A.D.1250)

F = number of fragments identified
M = minimum number of individuals represented.

* Cat includes 21 fragments from one burial.

Cattle	M	% Stock	M.R.B.	S.M.	Cat.1	Cat.2	Cat.3	Cat.4	Cat.5	Cat.6	Cat.7	Chi^2
GS I-II	4	36.36	f.	24	-	-	-	-	-	-	-	-
GS III	11	29.73	t.	86	0.19	0.34	0.23	0.10	0.05	0.06	0.03	A
HS	3	33.33	f.	17	-	-	-	-	-	-	-	-
TOTAL	18	31.58	-	127	0.18	0.35	0.20	0.11	0.06	0.07	0.03	

Sheep/Goat	M	% Stock	M.R.B.	S.M.	Cat.1	Cat.2	Cat.3	Cat.4	Cat.5	Cat.6	Cat.7	Chi^2
GS I-II	5	45.46	m.	36	-	-	-	-	-	-	-	-
GS III	18	48.65	t.	121	0.19	0.26	0.26	0.14	0.07	0.05	0.03	A
HS	3	33.33	sk.t.	19	-	-	-	-	-	-	-	-
TOTAL	26	45.61	-	176	0.23	0.25	0.25	0.14	0.06	0.05	0.03	

Pig	M	% Stock	M.R.B.	S.M.	Cat.1	Cat.2	Cat.3	Cat.4	Cat.5	Cat.6	Cat.7	Chi^2
GS I-II	2	18.18	t.	13	-	-	-	-	-	-	-	-
GS III	8	21.62	t.	65	0.31	0.15	0.20	0.17	0.08	0.08	0.02	A
HS	3	33.33	te.	7	-	-	-	-	-	-	-	-
TOTAL	13	22.81	-	85	0.31	0.16	0.20	0.16	0.07	0.07	0.02	

TABLE 25

Minimum number of individuals and category proportions
of the principal stock animals - phase Md5

M = minimum number of individuals.
M.R.B. = most represented bone(s).
S.M. = sum of minimum numbers.
A = sample within 5% level of chi-squared.
m = mandible; te = teeth; sk = skull; f = femur; t = tibia.

123

Species		GS I-II		GS III		TS		TOTAL Md6	
		No	%	No	%	No	%	No	%
Cattle	F	368	41.07	966	36.93	283	39.14	1617	38.18
	M	16	29.63	35	25.36	14	24.14	65	26.00
Sheep/Goat	F	405	45.20	1115	42.62	325	44.95	1845	43.57
	M	19	35.19	54	39.13	27	46.55	100	40.00
Pig	F	88*	9.82	408	15.60	88	12.17	584	13.79
	M	10	18.52	24	17.39	10	17.24	44	17.60
Red Deer	F	1	0.11	1	0.04	1	0.14	3	0.07
	M	1	1.85	1	0.72	1	0.72	3	1.20
Roe Deer	F	1	0.11	2	0.08	–	–	3	0.07
	M	1	1.85	1	0.72	–	–	2	0.80
Hare	F	5	0.56	27	1.03	5	0.69	37	0.87
	M	1	1.85	5	3.62	1	1.72	7	2.80
Rabbit	F	–	–	4	0.15	–	–	4	0.09
	M	–	–	1	0.72	–	–	1	0.40
Horse	F	5	0.56	17	0.65	4	0.55	26	0.61
	M	2	3.70	3	2.17	1	1.72	6	2.40
Dog	F	15*	1.67	3	0.11	2	0.28	20	0.47
	M	1	1.85	1	0.72	1	1.72	3	1.20
Cat	F	5	0.56	72	2.75	15	2.08	92	2.17
	M	1	1.85	12	8.70	3	5.17	16	6.40
Rat	F	2	0.22	1	0.04	–	–	3	0.07
	M	1	1.85	1	0.72	–	–	2	0.80
Rodent sp.	F	1	0.11	–	–	–	–	1	0.02
	M	1	1.85	–	–	–	–	1	0.40
TOTAL MAMMAL	F	896	100	2616	100	723	100	4235	100
	M	54	100	138	100	58	100	250	100
Bird	F	125	11.49	351	9.49	102	11.27	578	10.16
	M	25		58		21		104	
Fish	F	67	6.16	732	19.79	80	8.84	879	15.44
TOTAL FRAGMENTS		1088	100	3699	100	905	100	5692	100
TOTAL UNIDENTIFIED		957		3126		538		4621	

TABLE 26

Number of fragments and minimum number of individuals represented in phase Md6 (A.D.1250 - A.D.1300)

F = number of fragments identified.

M = minimum number of individuals represented.

* Pig includes 8 fragments from one burial.
  Dog includes 13 fragments from one burial.

Cattle	M	% Stock	M.R.B.	S.M.	Cat.1	Cat.2	Cat.3	Cat.4	Cat.5	Cat.6	Cat.7	Chi^2
GS I-II	27	33.75	h.	254	0.15	0.26	0.20	0.14	0.11	0.07	0.07	A
GS III	17	26.56	t.	190	0.20	0.29	0.16	0.11	0.10	0.08	0.07	A
TS	1	-	-	13	-	-	-	-	-	-	-	-
TOTAL	45	30.40	-	457	0.17	0.28	0.18	0.13	0.11	0.08	0.07	

Sheep/Goat	M	% Stock	M.R.B.	S.M.	Cat.1	Cat.2	Cat.3	Cat.4	Cat.5	Cat.6	Cat.7	Chi^2
GS I-II	43	53.75	r.	307	0.15	0.33	0.28	0.11	0.06	0.03	0.05	A
GS III	32	50.00	r.	287	0.11	0.36	0.29	0.09	0.03	0.02	0.10	A
TS	2	-	r.h.	11	-	-	-	-	-	-	-	-
TOTAL	77	52.03	-	605	0.13	0.35	0.28	0.10	0.05	0.02	0.07	

Pig	M	% Stock	M.R.B.	S.M.	Cat.1	Cat.2	Cat.3	Cat.4	Cat.5	Cat.6	Cat.7	Chi^2
GS I-II	10	12.50	t.	71	0.21	0.27	0.28	0.06	0.13	0.06	0.00	A
GS III	15	23.44	f.	99	0.24	0.36	0.15	0.11	0.07	0.06	0.00	A
TS	1	-	-	5	-	-	-	-	-	-	-	-
TOTAL	26	17.57	-	175	0.23	0.32	0.21	0.09	0.09	0.06	0.00	

TABLE   45

Minimum number of individuals and category proportions
of the principal stock animals - phase Pml
(excluding GS II F.264)

M = minimum number of individuals
M.R.B. = most represented bone(s).
S.M. = sum of minimum numbers.
A = sample within 5% level of chi-squared.
h = humerus; f = femur; r = radius; t = tibia.

143

Species		GS I-II No	GS I-II %	GS III No	TS No	TS %	TOTAL Pm2 No	TOTAL Pm2 %
Cattle	F	67	39.88	6	39	32.50	112	36.48
	M	4	21.05	1	4	21.05	9	21.43
Sheep/Goat	F	90	53.57	10	45	37.50	145	47.23
	M	12	63.16	2	5	26.32	19	45.24
Pig	F	8	4.76	3	8	6.67	19	6.19
	M	1	5.26	1	2	10.53	4	9.52
Red Deer	F	–	–	–	1	0.83	1	0.33
	M	–	–	–	1	5.26	1	2.38
Fallow Deer	F	–	–	–	2	1.67	2	0.65
	M	–	–	–	1	5.26	1	2.38
Hare	F	–	–	–	4	3.33	4	1.30
	M	–	–	–	1	5.26	1	2.38
Rabbit	F	–	–	–	4	3.33	4	1.30
	M	–	–	–	1	5.26	1	2.38
Horse	F	1	0.60	–	–	–	1	0.33
	M	1	5.26	–	–	–	1	2.38
Dog	F	–	–	–	10	8.33	10	3.26
	M	–	–	–	2	10.53	2	4.76
Cat	F	2	1.19	–	7	5.83	9	2.93
	M	1	5.26	–	2	10.53	3	7.14
TOTAL MAMMAL	F	168	100	19	120	100	307	100
	M	19	100	4	19	100	42	100
Bird	F	6	3.30	6	129	48.13	141	29.62
	M	4		2	15		21	
Fish	F	8	4.40	1	19	7.09	28	5.88
TOTAL FRAGMENTS		182	100	26	268	100	476	100
TOTAL UNIDENTIFIED		120		62	112		294	

TABLE   46

Number of fragments and minimum number of individuals
represented in phase Pm2 (A.D.1550 - A.D.1650)

F = number of fragments identified.
M = minimum number of individuals represented.

144

Cattle	F	% Stock	Cat.1	Cat.2	Cat.3	Cat.4	Cat.5	Cat.6	Cat.7	Chi^2
GS I-II	67	40.61	0.19	0.27	0.21	0.18	0.03	0.10	0.01	A
GS III	6	–	–	–	–	–	–	–	–	–
TS	39	42.39	–	–	–	–	–	–	–	–
TOTAL	112	40.58	0.18	0.29	0.21	0.13	0.07	0.09	0.03	

Sheep/Goat	F	% Stock	Cat.1	Cat.2	Cat.3	Cat.4	Cat.5	Cat.6	Cat.7	Chi^2
GS I-II	90	54.55	0.14	0.54	0.24	0.01	0.03	0.01	0.01	A
GS III	10	–	–	–	–	–	–	–	–	–
TS	45	48.91	0.04	0.53	0.38	0.04	0.00	0.00	0.00	
TOTAL	145	52.54	0.11	0.52	0.29	0.04	0.01	0.01	0.01	

Pig	F	% Stock	Cat.1	Cat.2	Cat.3	Cat.4	Cat.5	Cat.6	Cat.7	Chi^2
GS I-II	8	4.85	–	–	–	–	–	–	–	–
GS III	3	–	–	–	–	–	–	–	–	–
TS	8	8.70	–	–	–	–	–	–	–	–
TOTAL	19	6.88	–	–	–	–	–	–	–	–

TABLE 47

Number of fragments and category proportions of the principal stock animals

F = number of fragments identified.
A = sample within 5% level of chi-squared.

Cattle	M	% Stock	M.R.B.	S.M.	Cat.1	Cat.2	Cat.3	Cat.4	Cat.5	Cat.6	Cat.7	Chi^2
GS I-II	4	23.53	t.mt.	43	0.16	0.28	0.21	0.19	0.02	0.12	0.02	A
GS III	1	–	–	6	–	–	–	–	–	–	–	–
TS	4	36.36	s.h.c.	32	–	–	–	–	–	–	–	–
TOTAL	9	28.13	–	81	0.16	0.31	0.19	0.14	0.09	0.09	0.04	

Sheep/Goat	M	% Stock	M.R.B.	S.M.	Cat.1	Cat.2	Cat.3	Cat.4	Cat.5	Cat.6	Cat.7	Chi^2
GS I-II	12	70.59	h.	50	0.16	0.54	0.18	0.02	0.06	0.02	0.02	A
GS III	2	–	r.	9	–	–	–	–	–	–	–	–
TS	5	45.46	u.	29	–	–	–	–	–	–	–	–
TOTAL	19	59.38	–	88	0.13	0.48	0.28	0.05	0.03	0.02	0.01	

Pig	M	% Stock	M.R.B.	S.M.	Cat.1	Cat.2	Cat.3	Cat.4	Cat.5	Cat.6	Cat.7	Chi^2
GS I-II	1	5.88	–	7	–	–	–	–	–	–	–	–
GS III	1	–	–	3	–	–	–	–	–	–	–	–
TS	2	18.18	sk.t.	7	–	–	–	–	–	–	–	–
TOTAL	4	12.50	–	17	–	–	–	–	–	–	–	

TABLE   48

*Minimum number of individuals and category proportions
of the principal stock animals – phase Pm2*

M = minimum number of individuals.
M.R.B. = most represented bone(s).
S.M. = sum of minimum numbers.
A = sample within 5% level of chi-squared.
sk = skull; h = humerus; r = radius; u = ulna; t = tibia;
c = calcaneum; s = scapula; mt = metatarsus.

Cattle	F	% Stock	Cat.1	Cat.2	Cat.3	Cat.4	Cat.5	Cat.6	Cat.7	Chi^2
GS I-II	350	37.00	0.27	0.30	0.18	0.09	0.03	0.11	0.02	A
GS III	85	36.02	0.31	0.27	0.09	0.05	0.05	0.22	0.01	*
TS	10	–	–	–	–	–	–	–	–	–
TOTAL	445	36.90	0.27	0.30	0.17	0.09	0.03	0.13	0.02	

Sheep/Goat	F	% Stock	Cat.1	Cat.2	Cat.3	Cat.4	Cat.5	Cat.6	Cat.7	Chi^2
GS I-II	502	53.07	0.20	0.35	0.22	0.13	0.04	0.02	0.04	A
GS III	119	50.42	0.25	0.39	0.24	0.02	0.02	0.03	0.03	*
TS	9	–	–	–	–	–	–	–	–	–
TOTAL	630	52.24	0.21	0.36	0.23	0.11	0.03	0.02	0.04	

Pig	F	% Stock	Cat.1	Cat.2	Cat.3	Cat.4	Cat.5	Cat.6	Cat.7	Chi^2
GS I-II	94	9.94	0.35	0.39	0.14	0.09	0.02	0.00	0.01	A
GS III	32	13.56	–	–	–	–	–	–	–	–
TS	5	–	–	–	–	–	–	–	–	–
TOTAL	131	10.86	0.31	0.46	0.15	0.06	0.02	0.00	0.01	

TABLE 53

*Number of fragments and category proportions of the
principal stock animals - phase Pm4*

F = number of fragments identified.

* = sample significantly different at 5% level of chi-squared.

A = sample within 5% level of chi-squared.

Cattle	M	% Stock	M.R.B.	S.M.	Cat.1	Cat.2	Cat.3	Cat.4	Cat.5	Cat.6	Cat.7	Chi^2
GS I-II	17	29.82	f.	175	0.19	0.31	0.21	0.09	0.05	0.10	0.04	A
GS III	3	21.43	h.r.t.	32	–	–	–	–	–	–	–	–
TS	2	–	t.	8	–	–	–	–	–	–	–	–
TOTAL	22	28.95	–	215	0.19	0.31	0.20	0.10	0.06	0.11	0.04	

Sheep/Goat	M	% Stock	M.R.B.	S.M.	Cat.1	Cat.2	Cat.3	Cat.4	Cat.5	Cat.6	Cat.7	Chi^2
GS I-II	28	49.12	h.	265	0.15	0.34	0.21	0.15	0.06	0.02	0.08	A
GS III	8	57.14	h.	53	0.17	0.38	0.21	0.04	0.04	0.06	0.11	A
TS	2	–	p.t.	8	–	–	–	–	–	–	–	–
TOTAL	38	50.00	–	326	0.15	0.35	0.21	0.13	0.05	0.02	0.08	

Pig	M	% Stock	M.R.B.	S.M.	Cat.1	Cat.2	Cat.3	Cat.4	Cat.5	Cat.6	Cat.7	Chi^2
GS I-II	12	21.05	m.	82	0.33	0.35	0.17	0.09	0.04	0.00	0.02	A
GS III	3	21.43	f.	14	–	–	–	–	–	–	–	–
TS	1	–	–	5	–	–	–	–	–	–	–	–
TOTAL	16	21.05	–	101	0.30	0.38	0.20	0.07	0.02	0.00	0.02	

TABLE 54

Minimum number of individuals and category proportions
of the principal stock animals - phase Pm4

M = minimum number of individuals.
M.R.B. = most represented bone(s).
S.M. = sum of minimum numbers.
A = sample within 5% level of chi-squared.
m = mandible; h = humerus; f = femur; p = pelvis;
r = radius; t = tibia.

		Cattle		Sheep/Goat		Pig	
Roman		S.M.	Proportion	S.M.	Proportion	S.M.	Proportion
Category	1	268	(0.23)	221	(0.22)	265	(0.29)
	2	315	(0.27)	265	(0.26)	243	(0.27)
	3	181	(0.16)	280	(0.28)	151	(0.17)
	4	139	(0.12)	131	(0.13)	113	(0.12)
	5	110	(0.10)	57	(0.06)	48	(0.05)
	6	100	(0.09)	30	(0.03)	55	(0.06)
	7	36	(0.03)	22	(0.02)	34	(0.04)
TOTAL/Chi^2		1149 /	**	1006 /	A	909 /	A

Medieval							
Category	1	498	(0.18)	722	(0.23)	376	(0.26)
	2	741	(0.27)	914	(0.29)	371	(0.25)
	3	533	(0.20)	850	(0.27)	319	(0.22)
	4	326	(0.12)	453	(0.14)	207	(0.14)
	5	302	(0.11)	108	(0.03)	76	(0.05)
	6	177	(0.07)	87	(0.03)	65	(0.04)
	7	149	(0.06)	63	(0.02)	51	(0.04)
TOTAL/Chi^2		2726 /	A	3197 /	A	1465 /	A

Combined Roman and Medieval							
Category	1	766	(0.20)	943	(0.22)	641	(0.27)
	2	1056	(0.27)	1179	(0.28)	614	(0.26)
	3	714	(0.18)	1130	(0.27)	470	(0.20)
	4	465	(0.12)	584	(0.14)	320	(0.13)
	5	412	(0.11)	165	(0.04)	124	(0.05)
	6	277	(0.07)	117	(0.03)	120	(0.05)
	7	185	(0.05)	85	(0.02)	85	(0.04)
TOTAL		3875		4203		2374	

TABLE 55

*Comparison of overall Roman and medieval category proportions
of the principal stock animals (sum of minimum numbers)*

S.M. = *sum of minimum numbers.*

** = *sample significantly different at 1% level of chi-squared
    from the combined Roman and medieval data.*

A = *sample within 5% level of chi-squared.*

Cattle	A	% Stock	B	% Stock
Plough Animals*	46,066	–	10,124	–
"Animalia"	7,357	–	1,055	–
TOTAL	53,423	45.28	11,179	48.69

Sheep/Goat	A	% Stock	B	% Stock
Sheep	50,039	–	9,689	–
Goat	7,263	–	1,613	–
TOTAL	57,302	48.57	11,302	49.22

Pig	A	% Stock	B	% Stock
TOTAL	7,263	6.16	480	2.09

TABLE   56

Domesday records of livestock on the demesne lands of Devon and in the hundreds around Exeter.

A = animals recorded on demesne lands in the whole of Devon.
B = animals recorded on demesne lands in the hundreds of Crediton, Exminster, Cliston, Hairidge, Wonford, Ottery, St. Mary, East Budleigh and West Budleigh.
* *= Estimate based on eight animals/plough team.*

154

Stage	55 – 300			GS 300+			TS 300+			Rest 300+		
	A	B	C	A	B	C	A	B	C	A	B	C
Stage 1	0	0	132	0	0	19	1	0	13	1	0	13
Stage 2	0	0	132	0	0	19	1	1	12	1	0	13
Stage 3	0	4	128	3	1	15	3	1	10	1	1	12
Stage 4	10	21	101	11	0	8	6	0	8	3	0	11
Stage 5	17	33	82	11	1	7	6	0	8	6	0	8
Stage 6	18	66	48	11	4	4	6	2	6	6	2	6

Percentage of animals killed

Stage	55 – 300	GS 300+	TS 300+	Rest 300+
Stage 1	0.00%	0.00%	7.14%	7.14%
Stage 2 min.	0.00%	0.00%	7.14%	7.14%
max.	0.00%	0.00%	14.29%	7.14%
Stage 3 min.	0.00%	15.79%	21.43%	7.14%
max.	3.03%	21.05%	28.57%	14.29%
Stage 4 min.	7.58%	57.89%	42.86%	21.43%
max.	23.48%	57.89%	42.86%	21.43%
Stage 5 min.	12.88%	57.89%	42.86%	42.86%
max.	37.88%	63.16%	42.86%	42.86%
Stage 6 min.	13.64%	57.89%	42.86%	42.86%
max.	63.64%	78.95%	57.14%	57.14%

TABLE 57

Cattle: tooth eruptions data - Roman period

A = number of jaws failing to reach stage of tooth eruption.
B = number of jaws with inconclusive evidence.
C = number of jaws reaching stage of tooth eruption.

Specimen	P4	M1	M2	M3	n.v.	St.6
1	–	–	n	m	54e	A
2	–	–	n	–	50+e	A
3	–	m	l	k	48	A
4	–	–	–	k	48e	A
5	–	–	l	–	47e	A
6	–	–	l	j	47e	A
7	–	–	k	j	45e	A
8	–	–	–	j	45e	A
9	–	–	–	j	45e	A
10	–	–	–	j	45e	A
11	–	–	–	j	45e	A
12	–	–	k	j	45e	A
13	–	k	k	–	44e	A
14	–	–	–	j	44e	A
15	–	–	k	–	44e	A
16	–	–	–	j	44e	A
17	–	–	–	j	44e	A
18	–	–	k	–	42+e	A
19	–	–	–	g	40+e	A
20	–	–	–	g	40+e	A
21	–	–	–	f	37–40e	B
22	–	–	–	f	37–40e	B
23	–	–	g	–	37–40e	B
24	–	h	g	–	c.37e	C
25	–	–	f	–	c.30e	C

TABLE 58 (i)

*Study of wear patterns on cattle mandibles dated
to A.D.55 - A.D.300 (phases R1-R7)*

n.v. = numerial value of mandible (after Grant 1975).
St.6 = stage 6 of tooth eruption sequence.
A = P4 certainly in wear.
B = P4 possibly in wear.
C = P4 not in wear.
e = estimated value of mandible.
- = tooth absent from mandible.

Specimen	P4	M1	M2	M3	n.v.	St.6
26	g	m	l	–	49e	A
27	h	m	–	–	49e	A
28	g	l	k	j	45	A
29	g	l	k	j	45	A
30	g	l	–	–	45e	A
31	f	l	–	–	45e	A
32	f	k	k	j	44	A
33	f	k	–	–	44e	A
34	f	k	–	–	44e	A
35	g	k	–	–	44e	A
36	g	k	k	–	44e	A
37	f	j	–	–	c.40e	A
38	c	h	g	–	c.37e	A
39	g	–	–	–	–	A
40	f	–	–	–	–	A
41	f	–	–	–	–	A
42	f	–	–	–	–	A
43	e	–	–	–	–	A
44	e	–	–	–	–	A
45	e	–	–	–	–	A
46	c	–	–	–	–	A

TABLE 58 (ii)

Study of wear patterns on cattle mandibles dated
to A.D.55 - A.D.300 (phases R1-R7)

n.v. = numerical value of mandible (after Grant 1975).

St.6 = stage 6 of tooth eruption sequence.

A = P4 certainly in wear.

e = estimated value of mandible.

- = tooth absent from mandible.

Fusion Age		55 - 300		GS 300+		TS 300+		Rest 300+	
7-18 months		NF	F	NF	F	NF	F	NF	F
Scapula	DF	0	45	0	15	0	11	0	5
Humerus	DF	1	35	2	8	0	10	0	5
Radius	PF	2	38	0	10	0	9	0	6
Phal.1	PF	0	62	0	20	0	27	0	8
Phal.2	PF	0	45	0	19	0	8	0	7
% unfused		1.32%		2.70%		0.00%		0.00%	

24-36 months		NF	F	NF	F	NF	F	NF	F
Metacarpus	DF	1	41	2	8	5	17	0	3
Tibia	DF	2	20	0	6	4	7	0	6
Metatarsus	DF	0	32	1	15	6	10	0	3
% unfused		3.13%		9.38%		30.61%		0.00%	

36-42 months		NF	F	NF	F	NF	F	NF	F
Calcaneum	PF	3	8	3	4	1	4	1	1

42-48 months		NF	F	NF	F	NF	F	NF	F
Humerus	PF	1	5	0	0	0	0	1	2
Radius	DF	2	19	1	3	0	3	1	5
Ulna	PF	0	2	1	0	0	0	0	0
Femur	PF	8	14	3	1	3	5	1	1
Femur	DF	6	4	0	1	1	1	1	0
Tibia	PF	5	5	0	4	1	3	0	3
% unfused		30.99%		35.71%		29.41%		26.67%	

TABLE 59

Cattle: epiphyseal fusion data - Roman period

NF = not fused.
F = fused.
PF = proximal fusion point.
DF = distal fusion point.

Ageing data after Silver (1969; 285-6).

Stage	1000 - 1200			1200 - 1300			1300 - 1500		
	A	B	C	A	B	C	A	B	C
Stage 1	O	O	72	O	O	20	1	O	2
Stage 2	1	O	71	O	1	19	1	O	2
Stage 3	2	1	69	O	2	18	1	O	2
Stage 4	9	9	54	1	2	17	1	1	1
Stage 5	12	10	50	1	5	14	1	1	1
Stage 6	12	30	30	3	4	13	1	2	O

Percentage of animals killed

Stage	1000 - 1200	1200 - 1300
Stage 1	0.00%	0.00%
Stage 2 min.	1.39%	0.00%
max.	1.39%	5.00%
Stage 3 min.	2.78%	0.00%
max.	4.17%	10.00%
Stage 4 min.	12.50%	5.00%
max.	25.00%	15.00%
Stage 5 min.	16.67%	5.00%
max.	30.56%	30.00%
Stage 6 min.	16.67%	15.00%
max.	58.33%	35.00%

TABLE   60

Cattle: tooth eruption data - medieval period

A = number of jaws failing to reach stage of tooth eruption.
B = number of jaws with inconclusive evidence.
C = number of jaws reaching stage of tooth eruption.

Specimen	P4	M1	M2	M3	n.v.	St.6
1	–	–	–	m	50e+	A
2	–	–	n	–	50e+	A
3	–	n	l	l	50	A
4	–	m	l	k	48	A
5	–	–	–	k	48e	A
6	–	–	–	k	48e	A
7	–	–	–	k	48e	A
8	–	n	k	j	47	A
9	–	–	l	j	47e	A
10	–	l	k	k	46	A
11	–	–	–	j	45e	A
12	–	l	k	–	45e	A
13	–	–	–	j	45e	A
14	–	–	–	j	45e	A
15	–	k	k	j	44	A
16	–	k	–	–	44e	A
17	–	–	k	j	44e	A
18	–	k	–	–	40e	A
19	–	–	h	g	40e	A
20	–	–	h	g	40e	A
21	–	k	g	g	39	A
22	h	m	–	–	47e	A
23	g	l	l	j	46	A
24	g	l	j	j	44	A
25	g	k	k	–	44e	A
26	g	k	j	j	43	A
27	f	k	–	–	42e	A
28	f	j	j	g	40	A
29	c	k	g	g	39	A
30	c	h	g	g	37	A

TABLE 61

*Study of wear pattern on cattle mandibles dated
to the eleventh-twelfth centuries (phases Md1-Md3)*

n.v. = numerical value (after Grant 1975).
St.6 = Stage 6 of tooth eruption sequence.
A = P4 certainly in wear.
e = estimated value.
- = tooth absent from mandible.

Measurement		Date	N	Range	Mean	S	V
Radius	(1)	55-300	10	65.5-78.8	71.7	4.14	5.77
	(1)	300+	5	61.2-71.0	67.0	–	–
	(1)	1000-1150	16	60.3-85.4	68.8	6.02	8.75
	(1)	1100-1200	25	56.7-79.1	68.2	5.56	8.15
	(1)	1200-1300	16	55.1-79.3	68.5	7.91	11.55
	(1)	1300-1500	6	62.3-80.5	71.0	7.33	10.32
	(1)	1500-1700	3	66.0-80.6	73.4	–	–
Radius	(2)	55-300	3	58.0-60.5	59.3	–	–
	(2)	300+	6	59.2-76.7	68.8	6.69	9.72
	(2)	1000-1150	11	58.1-71.9	63.4	4.84	7.63
	(2)	1100-1200	13	54.7-69.5	60.1	5.74	9.55
	(2)	1000-1200	6	49.3-67.6	59.1	7.38	12.48
	(2)	1200-1300	11	54.0-72.1	61.4	6.51	10.60
	(2)	Postmed.	5	49.6-85.0	70.7	–	–
Radius	(L)	Roman	5	243-274	261.6	–	–
	(L)	Medieval	3	240-254	245.7	–	–
Metacarpus	(1)	55-300	30	44.8-57.3	48.8	3.70	7.58
	(1)	300+	31	43.7-54.0	47.9	2.14	4.47
	(1)	1000-1150	12	45.0-54.9	49.2	3.45	7.01
	(1)	1100-1200	35	42.3-57.8	49.6	4.66	9.40
	(1)	1200-1300	17	42.5-58.7	49.7	4.72	9.50
	(1)	1300-1500	7	45.1-52.9	49.6	2.91	5.87
	(1)	1500-1700	16	36.5-62.3	49.8	6.36	12.77
	(1)	1700-1800	4	39.5-51.0	46.7	–	–
Metacarpus	(2)	55-300	26	27.9-34.0	30.5	1.94	6.36
	(2)	300+	30	27.1-34.1	29.5	1.79	6.07
	(2)	1000-1150	12	27.9-34.2	30.4	2.15	7.07
	(2)	1100-1200	34	26.4-38.9	31.3	3.25	10.38
	(2)	1200-1300	15	25.2-38.6	32.3	3.84	11.89
	(2)	1300-1500	6	27.4-33.6	31.7	1.11	3.50
	(2)	1500-1700	15	21.2-38.2	31.1	4.46	14.34
	(2)	1700-1800	4	23.2-33.8	29.5	–	–
Metacarpus	(3)	55-300	36	40.9-52.9	45.3	3.55	7.84
	(3)	300+	26	38.5-50.5	44.8	2.73	6.09
	(3)	1000-1150	11	42.2-50.5	46.1	2.90	6.29
	(3)	1100-1200	26	39.9-55.4	47.0	4.54	9.66
	(3)	1200-1300	20	40.3-58.4	46.8	4.65	9.94
	(3)	1300-1500	4	41.4-53.2	46.1	–	–
	(3)	1500-1700	13	40.9-61.4	50.6	7.57	14.96
Metacarpus	(4)	55-300	35	20.6-27.2	24.2	1.48	6.12
	(4)	300+	23	20.0-27.5	24.1	1.83	7.59
	(4)	1000-1150	10	23.6-25.4	24.2	0.61	2.52
	(4)	1100-1200	26	21.6-28.1	24.3	1.95	8.02
	(4)	1200-1300	20	20.3-28.0	23.9	1.82	7.62
	(4)	1300-1500	4	22.0-26.0	24.5	–	–
	(4)	1500-1700	13	22.0-31.6	25.7	3.39	13.19
Metacarpus	(5)	55-300	30	44.5-60.6	48.6	4.69	9.65
	(5)	300+	19	44.3-55.0	50.0	2.41	4.82
	(5)	1000-1150	9	46.7-55.8	51.2	3.11	6.07
	(5)	1100-1200	22	43.2-62.5	52.8	5.68	10.76
	(5)	1200-1300	12	44.3-62.0	52.5	5.27	10.04
	(5)	1300-1500	3	45.9-58.0	50.2	–	–
Metacarpus	(L)	55-300	5	166-194	174.8	10.03	5.74
	(L)	300+	13	159-183	174.3	6.65	3.82
	(L)	1000-1150	4	167-174	170.0	–	–
	(L)	1100-1200	15	156-196	174.7	11.36	6.50

TABLE 65 (ii)

Metrical analysis of cattle

Key to measurements in Appendix I.
All measurements in millimetres.
N = number of specimens.
S = standard deviation.
V = coefficient of variation.

Measurement		Date	N	Range	Mean	S	V
Metacarpus	(L)	1200-1300	6	159-192	173.6	12.51	7.21
	(L)	1500-1700	5	153-213	183.8	-	-
Tibia	(1)	55-300	9	49.7-63.3	55.4	4.51	8.14
	(1)	300+	11	50.1-65.1	55.7	4.16	7.47
	(1)	1000-1150	21	48.7-62.2	54.0	4.11	7.61
	(1)	1100-1200	28	47.7-62.7	53.2	3.85	7.24
	(1)	1200-1300	29	46.8-60.4	54.4	4.09	7.52
	(1)	1300-1500	5	49.9-58.8	54.6	-	-
	(1)	1500-1700	9	48.6-69.0	59.0	6.73	11.41
Tibia	(2)	55-300	11	35.3-47.3	41.3	3.44	8.33
	(2)	300+	11	35.0-46.0	39.5	3.29	8.33
	(2)	1000-1150	21	35.0-47.1	39.6	3.55	8.96
	(2)	1100-1200	27	34.8-45.8	38.7	2.91	7.52
	(2)	1200-1300	29	33.6-47.0	39.0	2.98	7.64
	(2)	1300-1500	5	37.9-44.2	40.8	-	-
	(2)	1500-1700	8	32.5-46.9	41.5	-	-
Tibia	(L)	300+	3	284-311	293.7	-	-
Astragalus	(1)	55-300	14	50.7-59.6	55.2	2.59	4.69
	(1)	300+	18	54.3-62.0	58.3	2.48	4.25
	(1)	1000-1150	14	50.5-63.1	57.6	3.26	5.66
	(1)	1100-1200	17	52.2-64.3	57.6	3.96	6.88
	(1)	1200-1300	13	50.5-59.9	55.2	2.87	5.20
	(1)	1300-1500	3	54.5-58.0	56.0	-	-
	(1)	1500-1700	15	53.3-68.9	59.6	4.75	7.97
Astragalus	(2)	55-300	14	28.9-35.3	31.6	1.58	5.00
	(2)	300+	18	29.1-38.0	33.3	2.28	6.85
	(2)	1000-1150	14	29.5-36.3	31.8	1.97	6.20
	(2)	1100-1200	16	29.7-37.4	32.6	3.07	9.42
	(2)	1200-1300	13	28.0-34.9	31.8	2.10	6.60
	(2)	1300-1500	3	30.3-33.0	31.4	-	-
	(2)	1500-1700	17	29.5-42.4	33.9	3.44	10.15
Astragalus	(3)	55-300	13	47.1-54.6	50.5	1.94	3.84
	(3)	300+	18	48.8-61.6	53.6	2.93	5.47
	(3)	1000-1150	15	45.6-56.4	52.2	3.20	6.13
	(3)	1100-1200	17	48.4-59.3	53.1	3.35	6.31
	(3)	1200-1300	15	45.5-56.6	50.8	3.32	6.54
	(3)	1300-1500	3	50.1-51.9	51.1	-	-
	(3)	1500-1700	11	48.6-62.5	54.3	4.70	8.66
Calcaneum	(1)	Roman	5	37.3-46.3	42.3	-	-
	(1)	1000-1150	6	39.4-46.6	42.3	2.48	5.86
	(1)	1100-1200	19	38.0-46.5	42.9	2.31	5.38
	(1)	1200-1300	8	40.5-49.6	44.1	3.01	6.83
	(1)	1300-1500	4	36.5-45.2	40.0	-	-
	(1)	1500-1700	5	37.1-55.1	47.1	-	-
Calcaneum	(2)	Roman	3	21.1-25.3	23.7	-	-
	(2)	1000-1150	6	21.9-26.6	23.5	1.79	7.62
	(2)	1100-1200	20	20.7-27.0	23.3	1.67	7.17
	(2)	1200-1300	9	21.2-29.3	24.3	2.58	10.62
	(2)	1300-1500	3	20.6-27.3	23.6	-	-
	(2)	1500-1700	6	22.5-29.6	25.7	2.62	10.19
Calcaneum	(3)	Roman	5	40.3-50.3	45.2	-	-
	(3)	1000-1150	5	43.7-48.3	45.5	-	-
	(3)	1100-1200	13	43.6-51.1	46.3	2.35	5.08
	(3)	1200-1300	7	41.6-47.5	44.7	2.33	5.21
	(3)	1300-1500	3	40.6-46.8	43.7	-	-
	(3)	1500-1700	3	43.8-49.0	46.1	-	-

TABLE 65 (iii)

Metrical analysis of cattle

Key to measurements in Appendix I.
All measurements in millimetres.
N = number of specimens.
S = standard deviation.
V = coefficient of variation.

Measurement		Date	N	Range	Mean	S	V
Calcaneum	(L)	Roman	6	99.1-129	115.9	–	–
	(L)	1000-1150	6	111-131	121.3	–	–
	(L)	1100-1200	20	101-136	120.0	9.41	7.84
	(L)	1200-1300	8	108-136	118.4	10.51	8.88
	(L)	1300-1500	4	100-116	105.3	–	–
	(L)	1500-1700	5	101-156	129.2	–	–
Metatarsus	(1)	55-300	38	37.3-45.4	40.8	2.11	5.17
	(1)	300+	24	36.0-48.2	41.7	2.84	6.81
	(1)	1000-1150	5	38.3-46.4	43.0	–	–
	(1)	1100-1200	31	36.8-49.1	42.1	3.46	8.22
	(1)	1200-1300	26	34.4-45.8	41.5	3.18	7.66
	(1)	1300-1500	4	38.3-46.5	41.7	–	–
	(1)	1500-1700	10	31.2-49.3	43.3	5.34	12.33
Metatarsus	(2)	55-300	33	36.0-44.8	38.7	2.25	5.81
	(2)	300+	21	35.4-44.9	39.4	2.82	7.16
	(2)	1000-1150	5	35.3-46.1	41.5	–	–
	(2)	1100-1200	29	32.8-46.8	39.3	3.83	9.75
	(2)	1200-1300	27	33.0-44.8	39.7	3.05	7.68
	(2)	1300-1500	4	36.4-42.5	39.0	–	–
	(2)	1500-1700	8	27.6-46.4	41.2	6.68	16.21
Metatarsus	(3)	55-300	24	38.3-49.5	42.3	2.63	6.22
	(3)	300+	25	36.9-51.1	44.0	3.60	8.18
	(3)	1000-1150	5	41.9-50.0	46.0	–	–
	(3)	1100-1200	23	36.8-49.1	44.8	3.48	7.77
	(3)	1200-1300	13	38.0-53.6	45.6	3.59	7.87
	(3)	1300-1500	3	40.0-49.1	43.3	–	–
	(3)	1500-1700	7	43.6-51.9	47.3	2.75	5.81
Metatarsus	(4)	55-300	22	22.8-28.5	25.2	1.69	6.71
	(4)	300+	22	22.3-28.8	25.4	1.97	7.76
	(4)	1000-1150	5	24.3-29.9	27.0	–	–
	(4)	1100-1200	20	22.4-28.7	25.9	1.61	6.22
	(4)	1200-1300	10	23.0-28.7	25.6	1.92	7.50
	(4)	1300-1500	2	22.3-28.4	25.4	–	–
	(4)	1500-1700	8	25.5-30.7	28.0	1.69	6.04
Metatarsus	(L)	55-300	5	190-205	199.0	5.51	2.77
	(L)	300+	10	191-219	204.4	9.24	4.52
	(L)	1000-1150	2	198-200	199.0	–	–
	(L)	1100-1200	10	182-223	196.5	14.40	7.33
	(L)	1200-1300	5	182-205	193.0	–	–
	(L)	1500-1700	3	199-222	208.0	–	–

TABLE   65   (iv)

Metrical analysis of cattle

Key to measurements in Appendix I.
All measurements in millimetres.
N = number of specimens.
S = standard deviation.
V = coefficient of variation.

Site	Date	N	Range
Exeter	Roman	20	49.7-65.1
Exeter	Medieval	83	46.8-62.7
Exeter	Postmed.	9	48.6-69.0
Portchester	Roman	143	50-69
Corstopitum	Roman	78	45-68
Gadebridge Park	Roman	13	44-60

a) Maximum distal width of tibia

Site	Date	N	Range
Exeter	Roman	15	190-219
Exeter	Medieval	17	182-223
Exeter	Postmed.	3	199-222
Portchester	Roman	108	183-240
Corstopitum	Roman	67	181-244
Gadebridge Park	Roman	3	208-254

TABLE 66

*Comparison of the range in size of Exeter cattle with cattle
from some other Roman-British sites*

All measurements in millimetres.
N = number of specimens.
Data from Portchester and Corstopitum after Grant (1975: 401).
Data from Gadebridge Park after Harcourt (1974b: 256-7).

Date	N	Range	Mean	S	V
Roman	24	90-175	118.7	21.6	18.2
Medieval	76	88-189	131.7	26.9	20.4

a) Basal Circumference of Horn Core

Date	N	Range	Mean	S	V
Roman	7	85-130	111.9	18.2	16.3
Medieval	38	70-178	119.8	32.0	26.7

TABLE   67

Metrical analysis of cattle horn cores

All measurements in millimetres.
N = number of specimens.
S = standard deviation.
V = coefficient of variation.

a) Humeri, femora, radii tibiae

Date	Complete Bones	Total Fragments	Percentage Complete Bones
Roman	10	843	1.18%
1000-1200	10	1216	0.82%
1200-1300	3	724	0.41%
1300-1500	0	243	0.00%
Postmed.	4	700	0.57%
TOTAL	27	3726	0.72%

b) Metacarpi, metatarsi

Date	Complete Bones	Total Fragments	Percentage Complete Bones
Roman	45	440	9.28%
1000-1200	46	313	12.81%
1200-1300	23	186	11.01%
1300-1500	4	72	5.26%
Postmed.	23	229	9.13%
TOTAL	141	1240	10.21%

TABLE   68

Cattle fragmentation data

Stage	55 - 100			100 - 300			300+		
	A	B	C	A	B	C	A	B	C
Stage 1	9	0	38	2	0	44	5	0	20
Stage 2	27	0	20	13	0	33	12	0	13
Stage 3	32	3	12	27	1	18	16	0	9
Stage 4	32	4	11	29	1	16	16	2	7
Stage 5	35	6	6	34	2	10	17	3	5
Stage 6	40	6	1	41	2	3	22	3	0

Percentage of animals killed

Stage	55 - 100	100 - 300	300+
Stage 1	19.15%	4.35%	20.00%
Stage 2	57.45%	28.26%	48.00%
Stage 3 min.	68.09%	58.70%	64.00%
max.	74.47%	60.87%	64.00%
Stage 4 min.	68.09%	63.04%	64.00%
max.	76.60%	65.22%	72.00%
Stage 5 min.	74.47%	73.91%	68.00%
max.	87.23%	78.26%	80.00%
Stage 6 min.	85.11%	89.13%	88.00%
max.	97.87%	93.48%	100.00%

TABLE 69

Sheep/goat: tooth eruption data - Roman period

A = number of jaws failing to reach stage of tooth eruption.
B = number of jaws with inconclusive evidence.
C = number of jaws reaching stage of tooth eruption.

Estimated Age (Months)	55 - 100	100 - 300	300+
1-2	6	O	1
2-5	2	1	3
6-8	1	1	1
9-11	1	1	O
9-17	8	1	2
13-14	2	1	1
15-16	4	5	2
17-18	3	3	2
17+	3	1	O
19-20	3	2	O
21-22	1	1	O
23-24	1	7	2
25-26	O	4	2
25+	1	O	2
27-28	O	2	O
29+	2	1	1
31-33	O	2	O
33-36	3	3	1
36-42	1	O	O
42-51	2	4	4
51-60	1	O	O
60-72	1	3	1
72+	1	3	O
TOTAL	47	46	25

TABLE   70

Sheep/goat: tooth eruption data
employing Carter's method of analysis - Roman period

Method of ageing from Carter (1975).

Fusion Age		55 - 100		100 - 300		300+	
6-10 months		NF	F	NF	F	NF	F
Scapula	DF	5	15	2	21	3	5
Humerus	DF	4	13	8	26	6	12
Radius	PF	2	12	7	38	10	17
% unfused		21.57%		16.67%		35.85%	
13-24 months		NF	F	NF	F	NF	F
Phal.1	PF	O	14	3	20	O	6
Phal.2	PF	O	6	O	1	O	1
Metacarpus	DF	5	3	14	O	6	3
18-24 months		NF	F	NF	F	NF	F
Tibia	DF	8	25	12	36	5	17
% unfused		24.24%		25.00%		22.73%	
20-28 months		NF	F	NF	F	NF	F
Metatarsus	DF	9	7	8	4	3	3
30-36 months		NF	F	NF	F	NF	F
Ulna	PF	1	3	3	3	1	1
Femur	PF	7	4	10	3	9	3
% unfused		53.33%		68.42%		71.43%	
30-36 months		Nr	F	NF	F	NF	F
Calcaneum	PF	5	9	6	14	1	4
36-42 months		NF	F	NF	F	NF	F
Radius	DF	7	5	20	14	8	6
Humerus	PF	2	1	5	O	2	O
Femur	DF	4	4	5	2	1	O
Tibia	PF	9	4	9	4	3	O
% unfused		61.11%		66.10%		70.00%	

TABLE   71

Sheep/goat: epiphyseal fusion data - Roman period

NF = not fused.
F = fused.
PF = proximal fusion point.
DF = distal fusion point.

Ageing data after Silver (1969: 285-6).

	(Md1) 1000 - 1150			(Md2) 1100 - 1200			(Md1-3) 1000 - 1200			1200 - 1300			1300 - 1500		
Stage	A	B	C	A	B	C	A	B	C	A	B	C	A	B	C
Stage 1	4	0	31	12	0	93	16	0	152	8	0	68	1	0	26
Stage 2	20	0	15	38	0	67	66	0	102	16	0	60	5	0	22
Stage 3	27	0	8	71	0	34	118	1	49	35	1	40	10	0	17
Stage 4	29	3	3	74	7	24	123	15	30	42	10	24	12	2	13
Stage 5	29	4	2	80	8	17	130	17	21	45	13	18	12	6	9
Stage 6	31	4	0	93	8	4	146	17	5	62	13	1	17	6	4

Percentage of animals killed

Stage	1000 - 1150	1100 - 1200	1000 - 1200	1200 - 1300	1300 - 1500
Stage 1	11.43%	11.43%	9.52%	10.53%	3.70%
Stage 2	57.14%	36.19%	39.29%	21.05%	18.52%
Stage 3 min.	77.14%	67.62%	70.24%	46.05%	37.04%
max.	77.14%	67.62%	70.83%	47.37%	37.04%
Stage 4 min.	82.86%	70.48%	73.21%	55.26%	44.44%
max.	91.43%	77.14%	82.14%	68.42%	51.85%
Stage 5 min.	82.86%	76.19%	77.38%	59.21%	44.44%
max.	94.29%	83.81%	87.50%	76.32%	66.67%
Stage 6 min.	88.57%	88.57%	86.90%	81.58%	62.96%
max.	100.00%	96.19%	97.02%	98.68%	85.19%

TABLE   72

Sheep/goat: tooth eruption data - medieval period

A = number of jaws failing to reach stage of tooth eruption.
B = number of jaws with inconclusive evidence.
C = number of jaws reaching stage of tooth eruption.

Estimated	(Md1)	(Md2)	(Md1-3)		
Age (Months)	1000 - 1150	1100 - 1200	1000 - 1200	1200 - 1300	1300 - 1500
1-2	1	6	7	6	1
2-5	3	4	7	2	O
6-8	O	2	2	O	O
9-17	4	9	15	2	1
11-12	1	O	1	O	O
13-14	4	2	7	O	O
15-16	3	8	13	2	1
17-18	4	7	14	4	2
17+	O	O	1	1	O
19-20	3	2	6	4	2
21-22	O	6	7	5	3
23-24	2	15	22	6	O
25-26	2	10	17	4	O
25+	3	7	14	9	2
26-30	O	O	O	5	O
27-28	1	1	2	1	1
29-30	1	2	3	1	1
29+	1	1	2	3	4
30-36	O	1	2	O	O
31-33	O	3	3	2	O
33-36	O	2	2	1	O
36-42	1	3	4	3	O
42-51	O	4	4	6	2
51-60	O	3	3	7	2
60-72	1	3	5	1	1
72+	O	4	5	1	4
TOTAL	35	105	168	76	27

TABLE 73

Sheep/goat: tooth eruption data
employing Carter's method of analysis - medieval period

Method of ageing adapted from Carter (1975).

Specimen	P4	M1	M2	M3	n.v.	Estimate based on Carter's method
1	–	g	f	b	30	23-24 months
2	f	g	f	b	30	23-26 months
3	–	g	f	–	30e	24-26 months
4	f	g	g	b	31	23-24 months
5	–	g	f	c	31	24-26 months
6	–	g	f	c	31	25-26 months
7	e	g	g	c	32	25-26 months
8	g	g	g	d	33	25-26 months
9	g	g	g	e	34	45-51 months
10	h	–	g	e	34e	30-32 months
11	g	g	g	f	35	30-36 months
12	j	h	g	e	35	36-42 months
13	–	g	g	f	35	36-42 months
14	g	g	g	–	35e	36-40 months
15	–	–	g	f	35e	42-45 months
16	–	h	g	f	36	28-30 months
17	g	h	g	f	36	43-51 months
18	h	h	–	f	36e	42-51 months
19	–	k	g	f	38	51-60 months
20	h	k	g	g	39	36-42 months
21	g	k	g	g	39	45-60 months
22	–	–	g	g	39e	45-51 months
23	h	–	g	g	39e	51-60 months
24	j	l	g	g	40	60-70 months
25	j	l	h	g	41	63-72 months
26	j	l	h	g	41	72 + months
27	–	m	h	g	42	72 + months
28	l	m	k	–	44e	78 + months
29	–	n	m	m	53	78 + months

TABLE   74

Comparison of Grant's and Carter's methods of ageing
sheep mandibles on specimens from medieval Exeter

n.v. = numerical value of mandible (after Grant 1975).
Estimates of age of mandible based on method of Carter (1975).
e = estimated value of mandible.
- = tooth absent from mandible.

Fusion Age		(Md1) 1000 – 1150		(Md2) 1100 – 1200		(Md1-3) 1000 – 1200		1200 – 1300		1300 – 1500	
6-10 months		NF	F	NF	F	NF	F	NF	F	NF	F
Scapula	DF	5	13	6	30	18	48	9	18	6	14
Humerus	DF	4	32	24	55	40	103	35	72	6	21
Radius	PF	6	32	29	75	43	130	22	81	11	35
% unfused		16.30%		26.94%		26.44%		27.85%		24.73%	
13-24 months		NF	F	NF	F	NF	F	NF	F	NF	F
Phal.1	PF	0	10	1	19	2	38	2	19	0	6
Phal.2	PF	0	1	0	4	0	6	0	1	0	1
Metacarpus	DF	8	10	35	22	53	37	42	22	9	4
18-24 months		NF	F	NF	F	NF	F	NF	F	NF	F
Tibia	DF	16	20	35	46	62	80	34	72	9	21
% unfused		44.44%		43.21%		43.66%		32.08%		30.00%	
20-28 months		NF	F	NF	F	NF	F	NF	F	NF	F
Metatarsus	DF	11	10	31	25	44	39	26	18	8	7
30-36 months		NF	F	NF	F	NF	F	NF	F	NF	F
Ulna	PF	9	5	26	12	42	20	21	7	10	3
Femur	PF	9	3	26	11	43	18	27	9	7	3
% unfused		69.23%		69.33%		69.11%		75.00%		73.91%	
30-36 months		NF	F	NF	F	NF	F	NF	F	NF	F
Calcaneum	PF	3	6	12	13	18	22	4	11	3	3
36-42 months		NF	F	NF	F	NF	F	NF	F	NF	F
Radius	DF	20	5	63	14	94	26	53	18	19	7
Humerus	PF	10	2	14	9	29	14	14	1	6	1
Femur	DF	8	1	30	8	42	11	31	8	8	6
Tibia	PF	16	4	45	16	68	24	28	7	10	5
% unfused		81.82%		76.38%		75.65%		78.75%		69.35%	

TABLE 75

Sheep/goat: epiphyseal fusion data - medieval period

NF = not fused. Pf = proximal fusion point.
F = fused.   DF = distal fusion point.

Ageing data after Silver (1969: 285-6).

	1500 - 1600			1600 - 1800		
Stage	A	B	C	A	B	C
Stage 1	6	0	21	8	0	26
Stage 2	9	0	18	12	0	22
Stage 3	13	0	14	13	0	21
Stage 4	14	1	12	19	3	12
Stage 5	16	6	5	19	8	7
Stage 6	21	6	0	26	8	0

Percentage of animals killed

Stage	1500 - 1600	1600 - 1800
Stage 1	22.22%	23.53%
Stage 2	33.33%	35.29%
Stage 3	48.15%	38.24%
Stage 4 min.	51.85%	55.88%
max.	55.56%	64.71%
Stage 5 min.	59.26%	55.88%
max.	81.48%	79.41%
Stage 6 min.	77.78%	76.47%
max.	100.00%	100.00%

TABLE 76

Sheep/goat: tooth eruption data - postmedieval period

A = number of jaws failing to reach stage of tooth eruption.
B = number of jaws with inconclusive evidence.
C = number of jaws reaching stage of tooth eruption.

Estimated

Age (months)	1500 - 1600	1600 - 1800
1-2	2	0
2-5	4	5
6-8	0	3
9-17	2	2
15-16	0	1
17-18	1	1
19-20	1	0
23-24	1	0
25-26	2	1
25+	1	3
26-30	0	1
27-28	1	1
29-30	0	4
29+	5	5
33-36	2	0
36-42	1	0
42-51	2	3
51-60	1	3
60-72	1	1
TOTAL	27	34

TABLE 77

Sheep/goat: tooth eruption data
employing Carter's method of analysis - postmedieval period

Method of ageing adapted from Carter (1975).

Fusion Age		1500 - 1600		1600 - 1800	
6-10 months		NF	F	NF	F
Scapula	DF	–	–	3	19
Humerus	DF	12	77	11	87
Radius	PF	9	105	4	87
% unfused		10.34%		8.53%	
13-24 months		NF	F	NF	F
Phal.1	PF	4	15	2	13
Phal.2	PF	O	3	O	1
Metacarpus	DF	11	14	16	37
18-24 months		NF	F	NF	F
Tibia	DF	8	52	10	50
% unfused		13.33%		16.67%	
20-28 months		NF	F	NF	F
Metatarsus	DF	1	9	4	18
30-36 months		NF	F	NF	F
Ulna	PF	13	20	14	36
Femur	PF	3	16	10	17
% unfused		30.77%		31.17%	
30-36 months		NF	F	NF	F
Calcaneum	PF	14	14	7	19
36-42 months		NF	F	NF	F
Radius	DF	14	21	15	32
Humerus	PF	21	44	20	34
Femur	DF	18	38	25	25
Tibia	PF	23	22	20	22
% unfused		37.81%		41.45%	

TABLE 78

Sheep/goat: epiphyseal fusion data - postmedieval period

NF = not fused.   PF = proximal fusion point.
F = fused.   DF = distal fusion point.

Ageing data after Silver (1969: 285-6).

Measurement		Date	N	Range	Mean	S	V
Mandible	(1)	Roman	20	17.0–21.3	19.7	1.45	7.37
	(1)	1000–1200	11	18.5–21.4	20.1	0.75	3.73
	(1)	1200–1300	16	17.2–23.0	20.0	1.42	7.10
	(1)	1300–1500	7	18.2–22.7	19.7	1.55	7.87
	(1)	1500–1600	6	18.5–22.6	20.4	1.42	6.96
	(1)	1700–1800	9	19.4–22.8	21.3	1.21	5.68
Mandible	(2)	Roman	15	37.9–46.7	42.8	2.27	5.30
	(2)	1000–1200	9	35.3–46.3	43.3	3.17	7.32
	(2)	1200–1300	14	40.0–48.2	43.3	2.30	5.31
	(2)	1300–1500	6	38.0–45.2	40.7	2.54	6.24
	(2)	1500–1600	4	44.2–45.0	44.0	–	–
	(2)	1700–1800	6	41.1–49.0	44.5	2.94	6.61
Mandible	(3)	Roman	21	16.8–24.4	20.9	1.79	8.57
	(3)	1000–1200	25	17.8–25.5	21.4	1.78	8.31
	(3)	1200–1300	18	16.7–24.0	20.5	1.71	8.34
	(3)	1700–1800	4	19.1–23.3	21.1	–	–
Mandible	(4)	Roman	10	58.1–67.8	63.5	3.06	4.82
	(4)	1000–1200	5	63.3–68.9	65.3	–	–
	(4)	1200–1300	6	62.1–66.3	63.6	1.46	2.30
	(4)	1700–1800	4	55.6–63.8	60.2	–	–
Maxilla	(1)	Roman	4	17.4–22.8	20.1	–	–
	(1)	1000–1200	17	14.5–18.4	16.3	1.20	7.36
Maxilla	(2)	Roman	4	38.2–46.6	43.3	–	–
	(2)	1000–1200	13	38.1–42.9	40.7	2.04	5.01
Maxilla	(3)	Roman	6	20.0–26.6	22.5	2.55	11.33
	(3)	1000–1200	13	17.9–23.8	21.3	1.65	7.75
Scapula	(1)	Roman	23	25.9–32.1	28.4	1.68	5.92
	(1)	1000–1150	13	27.3–30.5	29.1	0.99	3.40
	(1)	1100–1200	29	27.3–32.9	30.0	1.34	4.47
	(1)	1200–1300	17	27.0–31.8	29.0	1.33	4.59
	(1)	1300–1500	9	28.8–33.1	30.4	1.33	4.38
	(1)	1500–1600	38	27.3–35.3	31.0	1.98	6.39
	(1)	1600–1700	28	28.7–36.6	32.4	1.92	5.93
	(1)	1700–1800	19	29.1–36.6	32.4	2.26	6.98
Scapula	(2)	Roman	19	19.0–24.9	21.7	1.36	6.27
	(2)	1000–1150	14	21.2–24.2	22.6	1.02	4.51
	(2)	1100–1200	28	21.0–26.5	22.7	1.24	5.46
	(2)	1200–1300	16	22.0–24.4	22.6	0.61	2.70
	(2)	1300–1500	8	22.3–24.9	23.6	0.83	3.52
	(2)	1500–1600	39	19.9–27.2	23.8	1.82	7.65
	(2)	1600–1700	28	21.0–28.2	24.8	1.61	6.49
	(2)	1700–1800	19	21.4–29.5	24.9	2.18	8.76
Scapula	(3)	Roman	19	15.9–18.9	17.5	0.90	5.14
	(3)	1000–1150	6	16.1–19.2	17.6	1.15	6.53
	(3)	1100–1200	16	16.3–20.1	18.2	1.10	6.04
	(3)	1200–1300	6	16.9–18.1	17.6	0.46	2.61
	(3)	1300–1500	8	17.5–20.0	18.9	0.78	4.12
Scapula	(4)	Roman	19	15.6–20.2	18.2	1.41	7.74
	(4)	1000–1150	6	15.8–19.1	17.5	1.60	9.14
	(4)	1100–1200	16	14.7–21.6	18.4	2.09	11.35
	(4)	1200–1300	6	16.6–20.3	18.2	1.38	7.58
	(4)	1300–1500	8	16.9–20.3	18.7	1.06	5.67

TABLE   79   (i)

Metrical analysis of sheep/goat

Key to measurements in Appendix I.
All measurements in millimetres.
N = number of specimens.
S = standard deviation.
V = coefficient of variation.

181

Measurement		Date	N	Range	Mean	S	V
Humerus	(1)	55–100	9	24.1–28.0	27.1	1.42	5.24
	(1)	100–300	14	23.9–30.1	27.0	1.70	6.30
	(1)	300+	8	26.8–29.5	28.0	0.61	2.18
	(1)	1000–1150	22	25.8–32.3	28.2	1.71	6.06
	(1)	1100–1200	39	24.1–32.1	27.6	1.48	5.36
	(1)	1000–1200	13	25.8–29.7	27.8	1.12	4.02
	(1)	1200–1300	41	25.4–30.6	27.8	1.28	4.60
	(1)	1300–1500	10	26.0–29.7	28.0	1.27	4.54
	(1)	1500–1600	54	24.3–32.2	28.1	1.92	6.83
	(1)	1600–1700	42	25.2–32.0	29.5	1.66	5.63
	(1)	1700–1800	31	23.9–35.3	29.5	2.54	8.61
Humerus	(2)	55–100	8	21.0–26.4	22.6	1.67	7.39
	(2)	100–300	8	19.9–25.3	22.4	1.82	8.13
	(2)	300+	6	22.9–24.8	23.9	0.63	2.63
	(2)	1000–1150	21	20.6–29.1	23.6	1.85	7.84
	(2)	1100–1200	35	20.9–25.8	22.9	1.20	5.24
	(2)	1000–1200	13	21.0–24.6	23.2	1.11	4.78
	(2)	1200–1300	37	21.2–26.0	23.0	1.22	5.30
	(2)	1300–1500	10	20.6–24.8	23.3	1.28	5.49
	(2)	1500–1600	53	20.7–27.3	23.6	1.48	6.27
	(2)	1600–1700	40	20.1–27.8	24.4	1.69	6.92
	(2)	1700–1800	27	21.5–29.7	24.9	2.05	8.23
Humerus	(3)	55–100	10	14.6–18.0	16.6	1.08	6.51
	(3)	100–300	15	14.8–18.4	16.7	1.40	8.38
	(3)	300+	10	16.4–18.7	17.3	0.74	4.28
	(3)	1000–1150	23	14.6–20.2	17.3	1.28	7.40
	(3)	1100–1200	44	14.9–19.5	17.0	0.98	5.77
	(3)	1000–1200	14	15.7–19.0	17.2	0.88	5.12
	(3)	1200–1300	44	15.1–18.6	17.0	0.76	4.47
	(3)	1300–1500	10	16.1–18.9	17.7	0.85	4.80
	(3)	1500–1600	59	14.4–20.9	17.4	1.39	7.98
	(3)	1600–1700	45	15.6–21.0	18.2	1.18	6.48
	(3)	1700–1800	35	13.3–21.9	18.4	1.61	8.75
Humerus	(4)	55–100	10	23.0–27.2	25.3	1.44	5.68
	(4)	100–300	16	23.3–28.8	25.3	1.38	5.44
	(4)	300+	9	25.8–27.5	26.7	0.63	2.36
	(4)	1000–1150	23	23.3–31.1	26.6	1.69	6.35
	(4)	1100–1200	43	22.9–29.9	26.0	1.38	5.31
	(4)	1000–1200	14	25.1–27.3	26.3	0.74	2.81
	(4)	1200–1300	44	23.9–30.2	26.3	1.29	4.90
	(4)	1300–1500	10	25.0–28.1	26.7	0.96	3.60
	(4)	1500–1600	62	24.0–30.2	26.5	1.51	5.70
	(4)	1600–1700	45	23.0–30.2	27.6	1.47	5.33
	(4)	1700–1800	35	23.1–32.3	27.6	2.08	7.53
Radius	(1)	55–100	11	25.4–28.4	27.0	0.95	3.51
	(1)	100–300	26	23.5–31.3	27.1	1.72	6.35
	(1)	300+	10	26.2–30.4	27.9	1.69	6.06
	(1)	1000–1150	20	24.4–31.0	28.7	1.98	6.90
	(1)	1100–1200	57	26.1–31.6	28.5	1.34	4.70
	(1)	1000–1200	19	26.4–30.3	28.5	1.41	4.95
	(1)	1200–1300	45	25.4–33.4	28.9	1.46	5.05
	(1)	1300–1500	22	26.2–31.0	28.5	1.36	4.77
	(1)	1500–1600	83	24.6–32.7	29.0	1.72	5.93
	(1)	1600–1700	53	24.9–35.7	30.1	2.27	7.54
	(1)	1700–1800	22	28.1–34.5	31.7	2.21	6.97

TABLE   79   (ii)

Metrical analysis of sheep/goat

Key to measurements in Appendix I.
All measurements in millimetres.
N = number of specimens.
S = standard deviation.
V = coefficient of variation.

Measurement		Date	N	Range	Mean	S	V
Radius	(2)	55-100	5	23.9-25.2	24.3	-	-
	(2)	100-300	11	24.0-27.9	24.9	1.19	4.76
	(2)	300+	6	24.2-27.7	25.7	1.40	5.47
	(2)	1000-1150	5	23.0-29.0	25.4	-	-
	(2)	1100-1200	10	23.9-28.4	25.9	1.23	4.75
	(2)	1000-1200	5	24.6-27.6	26.6	-	-
	(2)	1200-1300	13	23.4-27.4	25.4	1.19	4.69
	(2)	1300-1500	7	23.5-27.4	25.7	1.23	4.79
	(2)	1500-1600	34	20.5-28.5	25.5	1.50	5.88
	(2)	1600-1700	21	22.8-31.8	27.3	2.26	8.27
	(2)	1700-1800	9	25.4-31.0	28.5	1.87	6.56
Radius	(L)	Roman	6	131-151	139.3	6.05	4.34
	(L)	1100-1200	6	128-141	138.3	1.97	1.42
	(L)	1200-1300	4	128-143	135.8	-	-
	(L)	1500-1600	25	119-154	134.9	8.66	6.42
	(L)	1600-1700	15	125-155	139.1	8.91	6.41
Metacarpus	(1)	55-100	8	18.0-24.5	20.5	1.87	9.12
	(1)	100-300	16	17.8-27.0	20.3	2.14	10.54
	(1)	1000-1150	17	18.5-25.5	21.4	2.13	9.95
	(1)	1100-1200	38	15.9-22.8	19.9	1.69	8.49
	(1)	1000-1200	12	20.2-23.6	21.4	1.06	4.96
	(1)	1200-1300	34	16.9-22.5	20.7	1.37	6.62
	(1)	1300-1500	14	17.2-22.3	20.2	1.37	6.78
	(1)	1500-1600	29	19.5-24.2	21.8	1.46	6.69
	(1)	1600-1700	22	20.0-24.9	22.5	1.16	5.16
	(1)	1700-1800	26	19.4-26.7	22.5	1.90	8.44
Metacarpus	(2)	55-100	9	11.5-18.3	15.0	1.75	11.66
	(2)	100-300	17	13.0-18.4	14.4	1.39	9.65
	(2)	1000-1150	17	13.2-18.0	15.5	1.44	9.29
	(2)	1100-1200	38	11.3-16.4	14.4	1.47	10.20
	(2)	1000-1200	12	14.1-16.5	15.4	0.79	5.13
	(2)	1200-1300	34	11.0-16.7	14.8	1.26	8.51
	(2)	1300-1500	13	11.5-16.5	14.7	1.25	8.50
	(2)	1500-1600	28	14.0-18.1	16.0	1.18	7.38
	(2)	1600-1700	22	14.6-18.8	16.5	1.12	6.79
	(2)	1700-1800	26	14.7-19.1	16.7	1.21	7.25
Metacarpus	(3)	Roman	6	20.7-27.8	23.0	2.61	11.36
	(3)	1000-1150	9	21.3-30.5	24.8	2.49	10.04
	(3)	1100-1200	20	20.5-24.5	23.1	1.15	4.98
	(3)	1200-1300	16	20.9-26.4	22.7	1.46	6.43
	(3)	1300-1500	5	20.7-24.1	22.9	-	-
	(3)	1500-1600	11	21.7-27.6	24.5	1.66	6.78
	(3)	1600-1700	13	22.6-26.8	24.9	1.26	5.06
	(3)	1700-1800	21	20.6-28.5	25.1	2.01	8.00
Metacarpus	(4)	Roman	5	10.8-13.9	12.3	1.18	9.59
	(4)	1000-1150	9	11.5-15.9	13.0	1.24	9.54
	(4)	1100-1200	20	10.7-13.8	12.6	1.05	8.33
	(4)	1200-1300	15	11.1-13.4	12.2	0.64	5.25
	(4)	1300-1500	5	11.4-12.2	12.0	0.36	3.00
	(4)	1500-1600	9	10.7-13.3	12.2	0.76	6.23
	(4)	1600-1700	14	11.8-14.3	13.0	0.54	4.15
	(4)	1700-1800	21	11.0-13.9	12.9	0.80	6.20
Metacarpus	(L)	Roman	3	112-127	119.0	-	-
	(L)	1100-1200	10	105-123	114.0	4.99	4.38
	(L)	1200-1300	7	99-124	114.0	9.17	8.04
	(L)	1500-1600	10	96-124	113.4	7.52	6.63
	(L)	1600-1700	11	110-128	118.7	6.65	5.60
	(L)	1700-1800	19	102-128	118.7	7.54	6.35

TABLE   79   (iii)

Metrical analysis of sheep/goat

Key to measurements in Appendix I.
All measurements in millimetres.
N = number of specimens.
S = standard deviation.
V = coefficient of variation.

183

Measurement		Date	N	Range	Mean	S	V
Tibia	(1)	55-100	21	21.3-29.2	23.1	1.54	6.68
	(1)	100-300	30	21.4-25.9	23.3	1.21	5.21
	(1)	300+	15	22.3-27.0	23.9	1.25	5.22
	(1)	1000-1150	13	20.6-26.8	24.1	1.69	7.01
	(1)	1100-1200	29	21.0-28.0	24.2	1.41	5.83
	(1)	1000-1200	8	22.2-25.9	24.0	1.21	5.04
	(1)	1200-1300	61	22.0-26.9	24.3	1.12	4.61
	(1)	1300-1500	16	22.0-25.7	23.8	1.20	5.04
	(1)	1500-1600	39	23.5-31.5	25.6	1.78	6.95
	(1)	1600-1700	24	22.5-28.9	26.0	1.42	5.46
	(1)	1700-1800	17	22.9-30.4	26.7	2.22	8.31
Tibia	(2)	55-100	21	16.0-20.0	17.7	0.84	4.72
	(2)	100-300	30	16.2-19.4	17.8	0.85	4.75
	(2)	300+	14	16.8-19.9	18.5	0.79	4.26
	(2)	1000-1150	14	16.4-20.4	18.3	1.20	6.56
	(2)	1100-1200	29	15.7-20.5	18.7	1.04	5.56
	(2)	1000-1200	7	18.0-18.8	18.5	0.28	1.51
	(2)	1200-1300	61	16.9-20.1	18.7	0.79	4.24
	(2)	1300-1500	16	16.9-19.2	18.2	0.70	3.86
	(2)	1500-1600	39	16.7-25.0	19.3	1.45	7.51
	(2)	1600-1700	26	17.4-22.2	19.7	1.26	6.40
	(2)	1700-1800	18	18.1-23.7	20.5	1.54	7.51
Astragalus	(1)	Roman	13	23.6-32.9	26.2	2.64	10.10
	(1)	1000-1150	4	24.7-27.4	26.4	-	-
	(1)	1100-1200	14	23.5-27.7	25.8	1.51	5.85
	(1)	1200-1300	11	25.0-29.0	26.9	1.48	5.50
	(1)	1500-1600	14	22.1-29.0	26.6	1.93	7.26
	(1)	1600-1700	6	27.5-29.1	28.2	0.75	2.66
	(1)	1700-1800	7	24.5-31.3	28.2	2.47	8.76
Astragalus	(2)	Roman	14	12.8-17.0	14.3	1.11	7.76
	(2)	1000-1150	4	14.1-15.8	14.8	-	-
	(2)	1100-1200	14	13.1-15.9	14.6	0.82	5.60
	(2)	1200-1300	11	14.0-16.6	14.9	0.77	5.17
	(2)	1500-1600	14	12.2-16.4	14.9	1.14	7.65
	(2)	1600-1700	6	14.1-16.2	15.3	0.71	4.64
	(2)	1700-1800	7	13.7-17.0	15.2	1.42	9.34
Astragalus	(3)	Roman	13	22.3-30.2	24.9	2.33	9.37
	(3)	1000-1150	4	23.8-26.4	25.0	-	-
	(3)	1100-1200	13	22.8-27.1	24.9	1.23	4.94
	(3)	1200-1300	11	22.8-27.5	25.5	1.45	5.69
	(3)	1500-1600	14	21.4-28.0	25.5	1.70	6.67
	(3)	1600-1700	6	26.0-27.4	26.7	0.62	2.32
	(3)	1700-1800	6	23.6-29.6	27.2	2.39	8.78
Calcaneum	(1)	Roman	17	18.7-23.0	19.9	1.00	5.03
	(1)	1000-1150	6	19.2-23.3	20.8	1.56	7.50
	(1)	1100-1200	13	19.0-22.0	20.5	0.95	4.65
	(1)	1200-1300	7	18.0-22.1	20.3	1.44	7.09
	(1)	1500-1600	13	18.2-23.9	21.8	1.36	6.24
	(1)	1600-1700	11	20.6-24.6	22.6	1.30	5.75
	(1)	1700-1800	5	21.9-25.0	23.1	-	-
Calcaneum	(2)	Roman	17	10.2-13.0	11.5	0.65	5.65
	(2)	1000-1150	6	11.0-12.8	11.8	0.78	6.61
	(2)	1100-1200	12	10.5-12.8	11.8	0.85	7.20
	(2)	1200-1300	7	10.7-12.4	11.8	0.71	6.02
	(2)	1500-1600	12	11.4-14.3	12.4	0.89	7.18
	(2)	1600-1700	12	10.7-14.6	12.6	0.99	7.86
	(2)	1700-1800	5	12.0-14.4	13.0	0.98	7.53

TABLE 79 (iv)

Metrical analysis of sheep/goat

Key to measurements in Appendix I.
All measurements in millimetres.
N = number of specimens.
S = standard deviation.
V = coefficient of variation.

184

Measurement		Date	N	Range	Mean	S	V
Calcaneum	(3)	Roman	11	18.9-23.5	20.8	1.10	5.31
	(3)	1000-1150	6	19.2-23.4	21.1	1.52	7.20
	(3)	1100-1200	12	18.4-22.1	20.9	1.01	4.83
	(3)	1200-1300	6	19.4-22.5	20.9	1.16	5.55
	(3)	1500-1600	11	21.0-23.9	22.2	0.87	3.91
	(3)	1600-1700	10	21.2-24.8	22.7	1.12	4.93
	(3)	1700-1800	5	22.3-24.7	23.3	0.90	3.86
Calcaneum	(L)	Roman	17	46.6-55.7	50.5	3.16	6.26
	(L)	1000-1150	6	48.1-55.3	52.7	3.30	6.26
	(L)	1100-1200	13	45.3-55.6	50.3	2.82	5.61
	(L)	1200-1300	7	45.8-54.9	50.8	3.14	6.18
	(L)	1500-1600	13	49.0-59.6	55.0	3.03	5.51
	(L)	1600-1700	11	53.0-59.3	56.2	2.31	4.11
	(L)	1700-1800	5	55.5-62.3	58.8	3.11	5.29
Metatarsus	(1)	Roman	25	16.0-20.0	18.2	1.05	5.75
	(1)	1000-1150	8	16.3-19.5	18.3	1.01	5.52
	(1)	1100-1200	33	16.8-19.5	18.4	0.78	4.24
	(1)	1000-1200	7	17.3-20.7	19.0	1.32	6.95
	(1)	1200-1300	32	16.2-20.4	18.6	0.95	5.10
	(1)	1300-1500	10	17.3-21.0	18.3	1.16	6.34
	(1)	1500-1600	15	17.8-21.4	19.8	1.22	6.16
	(1)	1600-1700	14	17.5-20.8	19.2	1.13	5.89
	(1)	1700-1800	12	18.9-21.0	19.8	0.65	3.28
Metatarsus	(2)	Roman	23	15.2-20.0	17.4	1.02	5.87
	(2)	1000-1150	9	16.4-19.5	18.1	0.87	4.81
	(2)	1100-1200	31	15.8-19.5	18.1	0.90	4.97
	(2)	1000-1200	7	16.8-20.2	18.2	1.47	8.08
	(2)	1200-1300	30	15.4-19.4	17.9	0.91	5.08
	(2)	1300-1500	10	16.8-19.6	18.0	0.93	5.17
	(2)	1500-1600	16	16.6-21.6	19.2	1.50	7.81
	(2)	1600-1700	14	15.2-20.0	18.6	1.27	6.83
	(2)	1700-1800	12	18.3-20.1	18.9	0.69	3.65
Metatarsus	(3)	Roman	12	18.9-21.3	19.8	0.64	3.25
	(3)	1000-1150	9	19.3-22.2	21.1	0.90	4.27
	(3)	1100-1200	18	19.6-23.7	21.6	1.10	5.09
	(3)	1200-1300	13	19.9-23.7	21.6	0.97	4.49
	(3)	1300-1500	7	20.0-23.1	21.1	1.09	5.17
	(3)	1500-1600	8	19.9-25.7	22.3	1.85	8.29
	(3)	1600-1700	10	21.1-24.6	22.5	1.17	5.20
	(3)	1700-1800	7	22.0-24.7	23.1	0.93	4.02
Metatarsus	(4)	Roman	11	10.9-12.3	11.5	0.41	3.57
	(4)	1000-1150	9	11.5-13.2	12.6	0.57	4.52
	(4)	1100-1200	19	10.7-14.3	12.5	1.00	8.00
	(4)	1200-1300	13	11.5-13.0	12.3	0.49	3.98
	(4)	1300-1500	6	12.3-13.6	12.9	0.51	3.95
	(4)	1500-1600	8	11.5-13.2	12.4	0.65	5.24
	(4)	1600-1700	9	11.1-13.5	12.2	0.77	6.31
	(4)	1700-1800	7	11.9-14.5	13.2	0.86	6.52
Metatarsus	(L)	Roman	9	120-143	126.2	6.64	5.27
	(L)	1000-1150	4	117-130	123.5	–	–
	(L)	1100-1200	8	111-134	125.8	8.46	6.72
	(L)	1200-1300	5	111-123	115.8	5.72	4.94
	(L)	1500-1600	5	118-128	123.6	–	–
	(L)	1600-1700	8	116-129	122.4	4.37	3.57
	(L)	1700-1800	7	109-129	120.4	7.09	5.89

TABLE   79   (v)

Metrical analysis of sheep/goat

Key to measurements in Appendix I.
All measurements in millimetres.
N = number of specimens.
S = standard deviation.
V = coefficient of variation.

Stage	Age	55 - 100			100 - 300			300+		
		A	B	C	A	B	C	A	B	C
Stage 1	c. 2-6 months	1	6	47	3	0	58	2	0	44
Stage 2	c. 7-9 months	5	3	46	5	0	56	2	1	43
Stage 3	c. 10-16 months	8	7	39	7	5	49	2	6	38
Stage 4	c. 16-22 months	22	5	27	22	4	35	14	5	27
Stage 5	c. 24-27 months	27	16	11	27	20	14	15	18	13
Stage 6	c. 27-30 months	30	16	8	28	22	11	21	19	6

Percentage of animals killed

Stage	55 - 100	100 - 300	300+
Stage 1 min.	1.85%	4.92%	4.35%
max.	12.96%	4.92%	4.35%
Stage 2 min.	9.26%	8.20%	4.35%
max.	14.81%	8.20%	6.52%
Stage 3 min.	14.81%	11.48%	4.35%
max.	27.78%	19.67%	17.39%
Stage 4 min.	40.74%	36.07%	30.43%
max.	50.00%	42.62%	41.30%
Stage 5 min.	50.00%	44.26%	32.61%
max.	79.63%	77.05%	71.74%
Stage 6 min.	55.56%	45.90%	45.65%
max.	85.19%	81.97%	86.96%

TABLE 80

Pig: tooth eruption data - Roman period

A = number of jaws failing to reach stage of tooth eruption.
B = number of jaws with inconclusive evidence.
C = number of jaws reaching stage of tooth eruption.

Ageing data adapted from Silver (1969: 298-9).

Stage	Age	1000 - 1200			1200 - 1300			1300 - 1500		
		A	B	C	A	B	C	A	B	C
Stage 1	c. 2-6 months	3	0	103	0	0	40	0	0	17
Stage 2	c. 7-9 months	5	3	98	2	3	35	0	1	16
Stage 3	c. 10-16 months	11	7	88	7	3	30	2	2	13
Stage 4	c. 16-22 months	35	9	62	17	0	23	4	3	10
Stage 5	c. 24-27 months	49	36	21	24	8	8	7	7	3
Stage 6	c. 27-30 months	62	36	8	27	8	5	9	7	1

Percentage of animals killed

Stage	1000 - 1200	1200 - 1300	1300 - 1500
Stage 1	2.83%	0.00%	0.00%
Stage 2 min.	4.72%	5.00%	0.00%
max.	7.55%	12.50%	5.88%
Stage 3 min.	10.38%	17.50%	11.76%
max.	16.98%	25.00%	23.53%
Stage 4 min.	33.02%	42.50%	23.53%
max.	41.51%	42.50%	41.18%
Stage 5 min.	46.23%	60.00%	41.18%
max.	80.19%	80.00%	82.35%
Stage 6 min.	58.49%	67.50%	52.94%
max.	92.45%	87.50%	94.12%

TABLE   81

Pig: tooth eruption data - medieval period

A = number of jaws failing to reach stage of tooth eruption.
B = number of jaws with inconclusive evidence.
C = number of jaws reaching stage of tooth eruption.

Ageing data adapted from Silver (1969: 298-9).

| | | | 1500 - 1600 | | | 1600 - 1800 | | |
Stage		Age	A	B	C	A	B	C
Stage 1	c.	2-6 months	O	O	21	2	O	15
Stage 2	c.	7-9 months	O	1	20	4	3	10
Stage 3	c.	10-16 months	O	1	20	4	4	9
Stage 4	c.	16-22 months	5	5	11	11	2	4
Stage 5	c.	24-27 months	7	11	3	14	2	1
Stage 6	c.	27-30 months	9	11	1	14	2	1

Percentage of animals killed

Stage		1500 - 1600	1600 - 1800
Stage 1		0.00%	11.77%
Stage 2	min.	0.00%	23.53%
	max.	4.76%	41.18%
Stage 3	min.	0.00%	23.53%
	max.	4.76%	47.06%
Stage 4	min.	23.81%	64.71%
	max.	47.62%	76.47%
Stage 5	min.	33.33%	82.35%
	max.	85.71%	94.12%
Stage 6	min.	42.86%	82.35%
	max.	95.24%	94.12%

TABLE   82

Pig: tooth eruption data - postmedieval period

A = number of jaws failing to reach stage of tooth eruption.
B = number of jaws with inconclusive evidence.
C = number of jaws reaching stage of tooth eruption.

Ageing data adapted from Silver (1969: 298-9).

Fusion Age		55 - 100		100 - 300		300+	
12 months		NF	F	NF	F	NF	F
Scapula	DF	2	9	2	17	3	7
Humerus	DF	3	7	4	18	4	11
Radius	PF	2	4	5	13	4	12
Phal.2	PF	3	1	O	7	O	2
% unfused		32.26%		16.67%		25.58%	

24 months		NF	F	NF	F	NF	F
Metacarpal	DF	10	1	16	6	10	8
Tibia	DF	4	5	11	8	7	2
Phal.1	PF	9	10	5	9	13	7
% unfused		58.97%		58.18%		63.83%	

24-30 months		NF	F	NF	F	NF	F
Metatarsal	DF	3	3	15	9	10	3
Calcaneum	PF	15	O	10	1	5	1
Fibula	DF	3	2	3	O	1	2
% unfused		80.77%		73.68%		72.73%	

36-42 months		NF	F	NF	F	NF	F
Ulna	PF	6	O	8	O	4	1
Humerus	PF	4	1	4	1	5	O
Radius	DF	6	O	6	O	10	1
Femur	PF	10	3	8	O	8	1
Femur	DF	11	3	9	O	4	1
Tibia	PF	4	O	7	2	8	O
Fibula	PF	1	O	1	O	3	O
% unfused		85.71%		93.48%		91.30%	

TABLE 83

Pig: epiphyseal fusion data - Roman period

NF = not fused.
F = fused.
PF = proximal fusion point.
DF = distal fusion point.

Fusion ages after Silver (1969: 285-6)

Fusion Age		1000 - 1200		1200 - 1300		1300 - 1500	
12 months		NF	F	NF	F	NF	F
Scapula	DF	2	25	O	4	2	1
Humerus	DF	4	39	4	25	O	4
Radius	PF	6	37	2	30	1	9
Phal.2	PF	3	10	1	5	O	O
% unfused		11.90%		9.86%		17.65%	

24 months		NF	F	NF	F	NF	F
Metacarpal	DF	54	6	26	3	1	O
Tibia	DF	38	20	17	14	6	2
Phal.1	PF	12	8	13	9	1	1
% unfused		75.36%		68.29%		72.73%	

24-30 months		NF	F	NF	F	NF	F
Metatarsal	DF	29	6	27	9	7	2
Calcaneum	PF	21	1	16	O	3	O
Fibula	DF	O	3	O	2	O	O
% unfused		83.33%		79.63%		83.33%	

36-42 months		NF	F	NF	F	NF	F
Ulna	PF	33	1	18	2	9	1
Humerus	PF	13	2	6	O	3	O
Radius	DF	24	O	13	O	2	O
Femur	PF	26	4	11	3	2	O
Femur	DF	21	4	14	1	4	O
Tibia	PF	28	2	16	3	3	O
Fibula	PF	7	O	2	O	O	O
% unfused		92.12%		89.89%		95.83%	

TABLE 84

Pig: epiphyseal fusion data - medieval period

NF = not fused.
F = fused.
PF = proximal fusion point.
DF = distal fusion point.

Fusion ages after Silver (1969: 285-6).

Fusion Age		1500 - 1600		1600 - 1800	
12 months		NF	F	NF	F
Scapula	DF	0	0	0	0
Humerus	DF	5	10	6	3
Radius	PF	2	7	2	3
Phal.2	PF	2	1	0	0
% unfused		33.33%		57.14%	

24 months		NF	F	NF	F
Metacarpal	DF	9	3	5	0
Tibia	DF	9	2	6	2
Phal.1	PF	9	3	2	0
% unfused		77.14%		86.67%	

24-30 months		NF	F	NF	F
Metatarsal	DF	4	0	2	0
Calcaneum	PF	10	0	4	1
Fibula	DF	0	0	1	0
% unfused		100.00%		87.50%	

36-42 months		NF	F	NF	F
Ulna	PF	3	0	4	1
Humerus	PF	6	1	7	0
Radius	DF	3	1	4	0
Femur	PF	1	1	8	0
Femur	DF	14	2	9	1
Tibia	PF	16	1	9	1
Fibula	PF	0	0	0	0
% unfused		87.76%		93.18%	

TABLE 85

Pig: epiphyseal fusion data - postmedieval period

NF = not fused.
F = fused.
PF = proximal fusion point.
DF = distal fusion point.

Fusion ages after Silver (1969: 285-6)

Site	Date	N	Size Range (mm.)			
			27.0-29.9	30.0-32.9	33.0-35.9	36.0+
Exeter	Roman	17	17.65%	52.94%	29.41%	0.00%
Fishbourne	Roman	52	13.46%	44.23%	30.77%	11.54%
North Elmham	Saxon	96	2.08%	26.04%	52.08%	19.79%

TABLE   86

Pig: length lower third molar - comparison with other sites

N = number of third molars measured.
Fishbourne data adapted from Grant (1971: 386).
North Elmham data adapted from Noddle (1975: 256).

Measurement		N	Range	Mean	S	V
Measurement	I	12	128-192	156.9	17.04	10.86
	II	12	71.1-96.4	83.7	6.73	8.04
	III	14	61.1-90.5	75.0	8.75	11.67
	IV	11	76.4-93.2	85.4	6.70	7.85
	IX	14	66.1-92.8	78.1	8.79	11.25
	X	16	46.0-60.8	53.0	4.53	8.55
	XI	16	44.8-62.5	53.5	5.61	10.49
	XII	14	25.6-34.9	30.3	2.25	7.43
CI		9	51.79-59.69	56.52	2.70	4.78
SI		11	45.95-51.92	49.05	2.25	4.59
SWI		14	37.43-45.88	40.56	2.67	6.58
Mandible	(1)	27	52.1-70.9	61.6	5.62	9.12

TABLE   90

Metrical analysis of dog skulls found in TS F.316
(late seventeenth century)

All measurements in millimetres.
N = number of specimens
S = standard deviation.
V = coefficient of variation.
CI = cranial index.
SI = snout index.
SWI = snout width index.
Mandible (l) = length of mandibular cheek tooth row.

cranial measurements after Harcourt (1974a: 152-3).

Measurement		Date	N	Range	Mean	S	V	Shoulder Height
Humerus	(L)	Roman	1	107	–	–	–	344
	(L)	Postmed.	8	84.9–151	121.9	22.74	18.65	265–491
Radius	(L)	Roman	1	172	–	–	–	567
	(L)	Postmed.	10	83.6–160	125.6	22.86	18.20	285–528
Femur	(L)	Roman	1	102	–	–	–	307
	(L)	Postmed.	8	105–168	140.3	21.84	15.57	317–515
Tibia	(L)	Postmed.	9	112–176	136.5	22.05	16.16	336–523

TABLE 91

Dog: long bone measurements

All measurements in millimetres.
(L) = maximum length.
N = number of specimens.
S = standard deviation.
V = coefficient of variation.

Estimations of shoulder heights after Harcourt (1974a: 153).

Species		200-300		300+		Undated Roman	
		No	%	No	%	No	%
Domestic Fowl	F	45	71.43	162	75.35	24	63.16
	M	13		24	51.06	3	
Grey Lag Goose/	F	1	1.59	7	3.26	4	10.53
Domestic Goose	M	1		4	8.51	2	
Mallard/	F	-	-	9	4.19	3	7.89
Domestic Duck	M	-		4	8.51	1	
Woodcock	F	7	11.11	23	10.70	3	7.89
	M	3		8	17.02	1	
Teal	F	-	-	2	0.93	-	-
	M	-		1	2.13	-	
Partridge	F	1	1.59	-	-	-	-
	M	1		-	-	-	
Pigeon	F	1	1.59	3	1.40	-	-
	M	1		2	4.26	-	
Stock Dove	F	-	-	1	0.47	-	-
	M	-		1	2.13	-	
Raven	F	-	-	2	0.93	-	-
	M	-		1	2.13	-	
Rook/Crow	F	1	1.59	1	0.47	-	-
	M	1		1	2.13	-	
Jackdaw	F	-	-	5	2.33	-	-
	M	-		1	2.13	-	
Thrush/Blackbird	F	4	6.35	-	-	-	-
	M	3		-	-	-	
Oyster Catcher	F	-	-	-	-	3	7.89
	M	-		-	-	1	
Cuckoo	F	1	1.59	-	-	-	-
	M	1		-	-	-	
Smaller Wader	F	-	-	-	-	1	2.63
	M	-		-	-	1	
Large Bunting	F	2	3.17	-	-	-	-
	M	2		-	-	-	
TOTAL	F	63	100	215	100	38	100
BIRD	M	26		47	100	9	

TABLE   95   (ii)

*Bird: number of fragments and minimum number of
individuals - Roman period*

F = number of fragments identified.

M = minimum number of individuals.

Species		1000-1150 No	1000-1150 %	1100-1200 No	1100-1200 %	1000-1200 No	1000-1200 %	1150-1250 No	1150-1250 %
Domestic Fowl	F	204	72.08	352	65.19	108	72.97	33	64.71
	M	31	58.49	50	60.24	15		8	
Grey Lag Goose/	F	42	14.84	135	25.00	22	14.86	15	29.41
Domestic Goose	M	8	15.09	15	18.07	5		4	
Mallard/	F	1	0.35	3	0.56	2	1.35	-	-
Domestic Duck	M	1	1.89	3	3.61	2		-	
Teal	F	-	-	2	0.37	-	-	-	-
	M	-	-	1	1.20	-		-	
Wigeon	F	-	-	-	-	-	-	1	1.96
	M	-	-	-	-	-		1	
Woodcock	F	16	5.65	29	5.37	15	10.14	2	3.92
	M	4	7.55	5	6.02	4		1	
Oyster Catcher	F	-	-	1	0.19	-	-	-	-
	M	-	-	1	1.20	-		-	
Curlew	F	3	1.06	-	-	-	-	-	-
	M	1	1.89	-	-	-		-	
Smaller Wader	F	1	0.35	-	-	-	-	-	-
	M	1	1.89	-	-	-		-	
Pigeon	F	2	0.71	1	0.19	1	0.68	-	-
	M	2	3.77	1	1.20	1		-	
Stock Dove	F	1	0.35	1	0.19	-	-	-	-
	M	1	1.89	1	1.20	-		-	
Woodpigeon	F	-	-	1	0.19	-	-	-	-
	M	-	-	1	1.20	-		-	
Raven	F	2	0.71	13*	2.41	-	-	-	-
	M	2	3.77	3	3.61	-		-	
Rook/Crow	F	1	0.35	-	-	-	-	-	-
	M	1	1.89	-	-	-		-	
Sparrowhawk	F	10*	3.53	-	-	-	-	-	-
	M	1	1.89	-	-	-		-	
Thrush/Blackbird	F	-	-	2	0.37	-	-	-	-
	M	-	-	2	2.41	-		-	
TOTAL	F	283	100	540	100	148	100	51	100
BIRD	M	53	100	83	100	27		14	

TABLE 96 (i)

Bird: number of fragments and minimum number
of individuals - medieval period

F = number of fragments identified.

M = minimum number of indivduals represented.

* Sparrowhawk includes 10 fragments from one skeleton.
  Raven includes 10 fragments from one skeleton.

Date	NF	F	% NF
Roman	32	262	10.88
All 1000–1200	127	366	25.76
1200–1300	79	307	20.47
1300–1500	38	99	27.74
1500–1600	128	453	22.03
1600–1800	52	261	16.61

TABLE 98

Domestic fowl: fusion data

NF = number of unfused longbones.
F = number of fused longbones.

Fusion of longbones of domestic fowl occurs by c.6 months of age (Silver 1969: 300).

Measurement		Date	N	Range	Mean	S	V
Coracoid	(L)	Roman	11	46.4-59.3	52.5	4.39	8.36
	(L)	1000-1200	18	44.9-55.0	48.2	2.49	5.17
	(L)	1200-1300	19	46.0-57.5	50.6	2.93	5.79
	(L)	1300-1500	2	47.8-57.7	52.8	-	-
	(L)	1500-1600	48	43.2-64.7	53.0	5.97	11.26
	(L)	1600-1800	17	45.5-67.8	56.4	7.27	12.89
Humerus	(L)	Roman	14	60.5-75.3	69.0	4.99	7.23
	(L)	1000-1200	28	60.2-78.1	66.4	4.70	7.08
	(L)	1200-1300	14	59.5-78.1	68.5	5.41	7.90
	(L)	1300-1500	12	61.1-75.7	66.8	5.42	8.11
	(L)	1500-1600	41	57.3-83.3	67.9	6.82	10.04
	(L)	1600-1800	25	65.7-88.6	75.0	7.15	9.53
Ulna	(L)	Roman	8	59.9-76.7	67.2	5.51	8.20
	(L)	1000-1200	13	59.9-79.4	65.7	7.16	10.50
	(L)	1200-1300	16	57.4-77.1	66.0	5.62	8.52
	(L)	1300-1500	11	59.1-74.8	68.2	6.13	8.99
	(L)	1500-1600	43	56.2-85.5	67.2	7.43	11.06
	(L)	1600-1800	32	60.7-89.3	74.9	7.19	9.60
Carpo-metacarpus	(L)	Roman	7	36.3-43.2	40.0	2.29	5.73
	(L)	1000-1200	9	34.3-40.9	37.9	2.31	6.09
	(L)	1200-1300	9	34.6-39.2	35.7	2.13	5.97
	(L)	1500-1600	6	37.4-44.3	41.7	3.38	8.11
	(L)	1600-1800	10	33.1-57.0	42.0	6.43	15.31
Femur	(L)	Roman	11	67.9-88.0	76.8	6.32	8.23
	(L)	1000-1200	23	64.8-80.9	73.0	4.84	6.63
	(L)	1200-1300	33	65.4-84.0	73.4	5.19	7.07
	(L)	1300-1500	9	66.7-88.1	75.1	6.48	8.63
	(L)	1500-1600	47	65.5-90.7	77.7	11.99	15.43
	(L)	1600-1800	39	70.0-94.9	81.9	7.23	8.83
Tibiotarsus	(L)	Roman	1	119.1	-	-	-
	(L)	1000-1200	20	92.5-117	104.3	9.60	9.20
	(L)	1200-1300	22	90.3-117	103.0	8.18	7.94
	(L)	1300-1500	9	96.0-115	103.9	7.75	7.46
	(L)	1500-1600	43	89.8-137	108.4	13.05	12.04
	(L)	1600-1800	50	96.2-150	118.4	13.29	11.22
Tarso-metatarsus (spurred)	(L)	Roman	5	63.8-89.2	77.6	-	-
	(L)	1000-1200	7	61.0-81.4	75.3	7.29	9.68
	(L)	1200-1300	5	75.0-81.1	78.5	-	-
	(L)	1300-1500	1	77.4	-	-	-
	(L)	1500-1600	11	83.9-95.7	84.8	6.16	7.26
	(L)	1600-1800	13	73.1-102	88.8	6.64	7.48
Tarso-metatarsus (unspurred)	(L)	Roman	8	66.2-79.1	72.0	5.29	7.35
	(L)	1000-1200	16	60.2-75.5	65.4	4.62	7.06
	(L)	1200-1300	14	57.0-78.9	64.8	5.48	8.46
	(L)	1300-1500	3	60.6-65.5	63.8	-	-
	(L)	1500-1600	33	58.1-79.0	69.3	6.38	9.21
	(L)	1600-1800	12	65.1-83.1	73.9	4.84	6.55

TABLE   99

Metrical analysis of domestic duck

(L) = length in millimetres.
N = number of specimens.
S = standard deviation.
V = coefficient of variation.

Measurement		Date	N	Range	Mean	S	V
Coracoid	(L)	Medieval	4	67.0-79.8	73.7	-	-
	(L)	Postmed.	2	75.0-83.0	79.0	-	-
Humerus	(L)	Medieval	3	149-172	166.3	-	-
	(L)	Postmed.	3	168-185	174.0	-	-
Ulna	(L)	Medieval	1	167	-	-	-
Carpo-	(L)	Medieval	15	84.6-100.9	92.5	5.03	5.44
metacarpus	(L)	Postmed.	9	86.2-97.1	91.0	3.75	4.12
Femur	(L)	Medieval	8	78.9-85.1	81.5	2.70	3.31
Tibiotarsus	(L)	Medieval	4	141-151	145.5	-	-
	(L)	Postmed.	1	149	-	-	-
Tarso-	(L)	Medieval	18	80.0-93.5	85.8	3.82	4.45
metatarsus	(L)	Postmed.	3	81.9-89.6	85.8	-	-

TABLE   100

Metrical analysis of greylag goose/domestic goose

(L) = length in millimetres.
N = number of specimens.
S = standard deviation.
V = coefficient of variation.

Phase/Date	Total Fish Fragments	% Identifiable Fragments
R1 55-75	13	0.98
R2 75-100	6	0.30
R3 55-100	0	0.00
R4 75-150	0	0.00
R5 100-200	6	0.31
R6 200-300	8	1.09
R7 100-300	0	0.00
R8 300+	41	1.34
R9 Undated Roman	15	2.81
Md1 1000-1150	414	12.72
Md2 1100-1200	1466	19.72
Md3 1000-1200	264	14.13
Md4 1150-1250	36	8.67
Md5 1200-1250	179	17.00
Md6 1250-1300	879	15.44
Md7 1200-1300	2	3.28
Md8 1250-1350	33	6.17
Md9 1300-1350	79	6.39
Md10 1350-1500	121	25.26
Pm1 1500-1600	1440	22.61
Pm2 1550-1650	28	5.88
Pm3 1660-1700	250	11.24
Pm4 1660-1800	189	10.52

TABLE 101

*Number of fish fragments and percentage
of total identifiable fragments*

BIBLIOGRAPHY

Allison, K. J. 1958. Flock management in the sixteenth and seventeenth centuries. *Economic History Review* 11: 98-112.

Andrews, A. H. and Noddle, B. A. 1975. Absence of premolar teeth from ruminant mandibles found at archaeological sites. *Journal of Archaeological Science* 2: 137-144.

Armitage, P. L. 1977. *Report on the Mammalian Remains from Baynard's Castle, Blackfriars, London*. Unpublished Ph.D. Thesis: University of London.

Armitage, P. L. and Clutton-Brock, J. 1976. A system for classification and description of the horn cores of cattle from archaeological sites. *Journal of Archaeological Science* 3: 329-348.

Armitage, P. L. and Goodall, J. A. 1977. Medieval horned and polled sheep: the archaeological and iconographic evidence. *The Antiquaries Journal* 57: 73-89.

Baack, B. 1978. The economy of sixteenth century England. A test of rival interpretations. *Economy and History* 21: 29-39.

Beale, P. B. 1969. The freshwater fishes of Exeter and district. F. Barlow (ed.), *Exeter and its Region*: 90-96. Exeter University Press.

Bettey, J. H. 1973. Sheep, enclosures and water meadows in Dorset agriculture in the sixteenth and seventeenth centuries. M. Havinden (ed.), *Husbandry and Marketing in the South-West 1500-1800*. Exeter Papers in Economic History 8: 9-18.

Bidwell, P.T. 1979. The legionary Bath-House and Basilica and Forum at Exeter. *Exeter Archaeological Reports* 1.

Binford, L. R. and Bertram, J. B. 1977. Bone frequencies and attritional processes. L. R. Binford (ed.), *For Theory Building in Archaeology*. New York: Academic Press: 77-153.

Boessneck, J. 1969. Osteological differences between sheep and goat. D. Brothwell and E. S. Higgs (eds.), *Science in Archaeology*. London: Thames and Hudson: 331-358.

Boessneck, J. A., Driesch, A. von den, Meyer-Lemppenau, U. and Wechsler-von Ohlen, E. 1971. Die Tierknochenfunde aus dem Oppidum von Manching. *Die Ausgrabungen in Manching* 6. Wiesbaden: Franz Steiner.

Boessneck, J. A., Müller, H. H. and Teichert, M. 1964. Osteologische Unterscheidungsmerkmale zwischen Schaf (*Ovis aries* Linné) und Ziege (*Capra hircus* Linné). *Kühn-Archiv* 78: 1-129.

Boserup, E. 1965. *The Conditions of Agricultural Growth*. London: Allen and Unwin.

Bourdillon, J. and Coy, J. in press. The animal bones. P. Holdsworth, *Saxon Southampton: Excavations in Melbourne Street*. Council for British Archaeology.

Bowden, P. J. 1956. Wool supply and the woollen industry. *Economic History Review* 9: 44-58.

Bowden, P. J. 1962. *The Wool Trade in Tudor and Stuart England*. London: Macmillan.

Brain, C. K. 1967. Hottentot food remains and their bearing on the interpretation of fossil bone assemblages. *Scientific Papers of the Namib Desert Research Station* 32: 1-11.

Branigan, K. 1977. *Gatcombe: the excavation and study of a Romano-British villa estate 1967-1976*. British Archaeological Reports (British Series) 44.

Branigan, K. and King, J. E. 1965. A Roman cat from Latimer Villa, Chesham. *Annals and Magazine of Natural History* 8: 451-463.

Bramwell, D. 1975. The bird bones. C. Platt and R. Coleman-Smith, *Excavations in Medieval Southampton*. Leicester: University of Leicester Press, Vol. I: 340-341.

Bridbury, A. R. 1974. Sixteenth century farming. *Economic History Review* 27: 538-556.

Bull, G. B. G. 1956. Thomas Milne's land utilization map of the London area in 1800. *Geographical Journal* 122: 25-30.

Carter, H. H. 1975. A guide to the rates of toothwear in English lowland sheep. *Journal of Archaeological Science* 2: 231-233.

Carus-Wilson, E. M. 1954. An industrial revolution of the thirteenth century. E. M. Carus-Wilson (ed.), *Essays in Economic History, Vol. I*. London: Arnold: 41-60.

Carus-Wilson, E. M. 1963. *The Expansion of Exeter at the Close of the Middle Ages*. Exeter: Exeter University Press.

Casteel, R. W. 1977. Characterization of faunal assemblages and the minimum number of individuals determined from paired elements: continuing problems in archaeology. *Journal of Archaeological Science* 4: 125-134.

Casteel, R. W. 1976. *Fish Remains in Archaeology*. London: Academic Press.

Chaplin, R. E. 1971. *The Study of Animal Bones from Archaeological Sites*. London: Seminar Press.

Clarkson, L. A. 1966. The leather crafts in Tudor and Stuart England. *Agricultural History Review* 14: 25-39.

Clarkson, L. A. 1971. *The Pre-Industrial Economy in England 1500-1750*. London: Batsford.

Clason, A. T. 1967. Animal and man in Holland's past. *Palaeohistoria* 13, vol. A.

Clason, A. T. and Prummel, W. 1977. Collecting, sieving and archaeological research. *Journal of Archaeological Science* 4: 171-175.

Clutton-Brock, J. 1976. George Garrard's livestock models. *Agricultural History Review* 24: 18-29.

Collis, J. R. 1972. *Exeter Excavations: The Guildhall Site*. Exeter: Exeter University Press.

Corfield, P. 1976. Urban development in England and Wales in the sixteenth and seventeenth centuries. D. C. Coleman and A. H. John (eds.), *Trade, Government and Economy in Pre-Industrial England*. London: Weidenfeld and Nicolson: 214-247.

Couch, J. 1878. *A History of the Fishes of the British Islands*. London: Bell.

Coy, J. P. 1977. *Bones of Birds and Non-Domestic Species from Melbourne Street sites I, IV, V, VI and XX of Saxon Southampton (Hamwih)*. Ancient Monuments Laboratory Report No. 2323.

Cram, C. L. 1967. Report on the animal bones. P. Salway, Excavations at Hockwold-cum-Wilton, Norfolk, 1961-2, *Proceedings of the Cambridge Antiquarian Society* 80: 75-80.

Cram, C. L. 1978. Animal bones. A. C. C. Brodribb, A. R. Hands and D. R. Walker, *Excavations at Shakenoak Farm, near Wilcote, Oxfordshire: part V Sites K and E*. Oxford: British Archaeological Reports.

Cutting, C. L. 1955. *Fish Saving*. London: Leonard Hill.

Davies, R. W. 1971. The Roman Military diet. *Britannia* 2: 122-141.

Doney, J. M., Ryder, M. L., Gunn, R. G. and Grubb, P. 1974. Colour, conformation, affinities, fleece and patterns of inheritance of the Soay sheep. P. A. Jewell, C. Milner and J. Morton Boyd (eds.), *Island Survivors: The Ecology of the Soay Sheep of St. Kilda*. London: Athlone Press: 88-125.

Driesch, A. von den. 1976. *A Guide to the Measurement of Animal Bones from Archaeological Sites*. Peabody Museum Bulletin, 1. Harvard: Peabody Museum.

Driesch, A. von den and Boessneck, J. A. 1974. Kritische Ammerkungen zur Widerristhohenberechnung aus Langenmassen vor-und frühgeschichtlicher Tierknochen. *Säugetierkundliche Mitteilungen* 22: 325-348.

Drummond, J. C. and Wilbraham, A. 1957. *The Englishman's Food*. London: Cape.

Dyer, A. D. 1973. *The City of Worcester in the Sixteenth Century*. Leicester: Leicester University Press.

Eastham, A. 1971. The bird bones. B. Cunliffe (ed.), *Excavations at Fishbourne 1961-1969*. Reports of the Research Committee, Society of Antiquaries of London, 27, vol. II: 388-393.

Eastham, A. 1975. The bird bones. B. Cunliffe (ed.), *Excavations at Portchester Castle, vol I: Roman*. Reports of the Research Committee, Society of Antiquaries of London 32: 409-415.

Ekman, J. 1973. Early Medieval Lund: the fauna and landscape. *Archaeologica Lundensia* 5.

Ewbank, J. M., Phillipson, D. W., Whitehouse, R. D. and Higgs, E. S. 1964. Sheep in the Iron Age: a method of study. *Proceedings of the Prehistoric Society* 30: 423-426.

Finberg, H. P. R. 1951. *Tavistock Abbey*. Cambridge: Cambridge University Press.

Fisher, F. J. 1954. The development of the London food market, 1540-1640. E. M. Carus-Wilson (ed.), *Essays in Economic History Vol. I*. London: Arnold: 135-151.

Fock, J. 1966. *Metrische Untersungen an Metapodien Einiger Europäischer Rinderrassen*. Gedruckt mit Genehmigung der Tierärzlichen Fakultät der Universität Munchen.

Fraser, R. 1794. *General View of the County of Devon*. Board of Agriculture County Reports.

Gamble, C. 1978. Optimising information from studies of faunal remains. J. F. Cherry, C. Gamble and S. Shennan (eds.), *Sampling in Contemporary British Archaeology*. British Archaeological Reports (British Series), 50: 321-353.

Grant, A. 1971. The animal bones. B. Cunliffe (ed.) *Excavations at Fishbourne 1961-1969*. Reports of the Research Committee, Society of Antiquaries of London, 27, vol. II: 377-388.

Grant, A. 1975. The animal bones. B. Cunliffe (ed.), *Excavations at Portchester Castle, vol. I Roman*. Reports of the Research Committee, Society of Antiquaries of London, 32: 378-408; 437-450.

Grant, A. 1976. Animal bones. B. Cunliffe (ed.), *Excavations at Portchester Castle, vol. II Saxon*. Reports of the Research Committee, Society of Antiquaries of London, 33: 262-287.

Grayson, D. K. 1973 On the methodology of faunal analysis. *American Antiquity* 38: 432-439.

Grigson, C. 1974. The craniology and relationships of four species of *Bos*. 1. Basic craniology: *Bos taurus* and its absolute size. *Journal of Archaeological Science* 1: 353-379.

Grigson, C. 1975. The craniology and relationships of four species of *Bos*. 2. Basic craniology: *Bos taurus* L. Proportions and angles. *Journal of Archaeological Science* 2 109-128.

Grigson, C. 1978. The craniology and relationships of four species of *Bos*. 3. Basic craniology. *Bos taurus* L. sagittal profiles and other non-measurable characters. *Journal of Archaeological Science* 3:115-136.

Grigson, C. 1978. The craniology and relationships of four species of *Bos*. 4. The relationship between *Bos primigenius* Boj. and *B. taurus* L. and its implication for the phylogeny of the domestic breeds. *Journal of Archaeological Science* 5: 123-152.

Halliday, F. E. (ed.) 1953. *Richard Carew of Antony: 1555-1620*. London: Melrose Press.

Harcourt, R. A. 1974a. The dog in prehistoric and early historic Britain. *Journal of Archaeological Science* 1: 151-176.

Harcourt, R. A. 1974b. Report on the animal bones. D. S. Neal (ed.), *The Excavation of the Roman Villa, Gadebridge Park, Hemel Hempstead 1963-1968*. Reports of the Research Committee, Society of Antiquaries of London, 31: 256-262.

Heinzel, H., Fitter, R. S. R. and Parslow, J. L. F. 1972. *The Birds of Britain and Europe*. London: Collins.

Higham, C. F. W. 1967. Stock rearing as a cultural factor in prehistoric Europe. *Proceedings of the Prehistoric Society* 33: 84-103.

Higham, C. F. W. 1969. The metrical attributes of two samples of bovine limb bones. *Journal of Zoology* 157: 63-74.

Higham, C. F. W. and Message, M. A. 1969. An assessment of a prehistoric technique of bovine husbandry. D. Brothwell and E. S. Higgs (eds.), *Science in Archaeology*. London: Thames and Hudson: 315-330.

Hodgson, G. W. I. 1969. Some difficulties of interpreting the metrical data derived from the remains of cattle at the Roman settlement of Corstopitum. P. J. Ucko and G. W. Dimbleby (eds.), *The Domestication and Exploitation of Plants and Animals*. London: Duckworth: 347-353.

Hodgson, G. W. I. 1977. *The Animal Remains from Excavations at Vindolanda 1970-1975*. Hexham: Vindolanda Trust.

Holderness, B. A. 1976. *Pre-Industrial England: Economy and Society from 1500-1750*. London: Dent and Sons.

Hoskins, W. G. 1935. *Industry, Trade and People in Exeter 1688-1800*. Manchester: Manchester University Press.

Hoskins, W. G. 1954. *Devon*. London: Collins.

Hoskins, W. G. 1956. English provincial towns in the early sixteenth century. *Transactions of the Royal Historical Society*, 5th series, 6: 1-19.

Hoskins, W. G. 1969. *Two Thousand Years in Exeter*. London: Phillimore.

Hoskins, W. G. and Finberg, H. P. R. 1952. *Devonshire Studies*. London: Cape.

Howard, M. 1963. The metrical determination of the metapodials and skulls of cattle. A. E. Mourant and F. E. Zeuner (eds.), *Man and Cattle*. Royal Anthropological Society Occasional Paper, 18: 92-100.

Innis, H. A. 1940. *The Cod Fisheries*. New Haven: Yale University Press.

Jewell, P. A. 1963. Cattle from British archaeological sites. A. E. Mourant and F. E. Zeuner (eds.), *Man and Cattle*. Royal Anthropological Society Occasional Paper, 18: 80-91.

John, A. H. 1976. English agricultural improvement and grain exports,1660-1765. D. C. Coleman and A. H. John (eds.), *Trade, Government and Economy in Pre-Industrial England*. London: Weidenfeld and Nicolson: 45-67.

Jones, E. L. 1968. The condition of English agriculture 1500-1640. *Economic History Review* 21: 614-619.

Jones, H. 1892. Note on the animal remains. G. E. Fox, Excavations on the site of the Roman city at Silchester, *Archaeologia* 53: 285-288.

Kennedy, M. 1969. *The Sea Anglers Fishes* 2nd ed. London: Stanley Paul.

Kerridge, E. 1967. *The Agricultural Revolution*. London: Allen and Unwin.

Lloyd, T. H. 1977. *The English Wool Trade in the Middle Ages*. Cambridge: Cambridge University Press.

MacCaffrey, W. T. 1958. *Exeter, 1540-1640*. Cambridge: Harvard University Press.

Maltby, J.M. 1977. *The Animal Remains from the Excavations in the City of Exeter*. Unpublished M. A. Thesis: University of Sheffield.

Marine Biological Association. 1957. *Plymouth Marine Fauna* 3rd ed.

Marples, B. J. 1974. Report on the animal bones. S. S. Frere and J. K. St. Joseph, The Roman fort at Longthorpe. *Britannia* 5: 122-128.

Marshall, W. 1796. *The Rural Economy of the West of England*. London.

Matheson, C. 1941. The rabbit and hare in Wales. *Antiquity* 15: 371-381.

Miller, E. and Hatcher, J. 1978. *Medieval England: Rural Society and Economic Change 1086-1348*. London: Longman.

Noddle, B. A. 1974a. The animal bones. C. Platt and R. Coleman-Smith, *Excavations in Medieval Southampton 1953-1969*. Leicester: Leicester University Press, vol. I : 332-339.

Noddle, B. A. 1974b. The early history of sheep. *Ark* 1, part 2: 14-15.

Noddle, B. A. 1975. A comparison of the animal bones from eight medieval sites in southern Britain. A. T. Clason (ed.), *Archaeozoological Studies*. Amsterdam: Elsevier: 332-339.

Noddle, B. A. 1976. Report on the animal bones from Walton, Aylesbury, M. Farley, Saxon and medieval Walton, Aylesbury: excavations 1973-4. *Records of Buckinghamshire* 20: 269-287.

Noddle, B. A. 1977. Mammal bone. H. Clarke and A. Carter, *Excavations in King's Lynn 1963-1970*. The Society for Medieval Archaeology Monograph Series, 7: 378-399.

Oschinsky, D. 1971. *Walter of Henley*. Oxford: Clarendon Press.

Page, W. (ed.) 1906. *The Victoria History of the County of Devon* vol. I. London: Constable.

Payne, S. 1972a. Partial recovery and sample bias: the results of some sieving experiments. E. S. Higgs (ed.), *Papers in Economic Prehistory*. Cambridge: Cambridge University Press: 49-64.

Payne, S. 1972b. On the interpretation of bone samples from archaeological sites. E. S. Higgs (ed.), *Papers in Economic Prehistory*. Cambridge: Cambridge University Press: 65-81.

Payne, S. 1973. Kill off patterns in sheep and goats: the mandibles from Asvan Kale. *Anatolian Studies* 23: 281-303.

Payne, S. 1975. Partial recovery and sampling bias. A. T. Clason (ed.), *Archaeozoological Studies*. Amsterdam: Elsevier: 7-17.

Pendrill, C. 1925. *London Life in the Fourteenth Century*. London: Allen and Unwin.

Postan, M. M. 1973. *Essays on Medieval Agriculture and General Problems of the Medieval Economy*. Cambridge: Cambridge University Press.

Power, E. 1941. *The Wool Trade in English Medieval History*. Oxford: Oxford University Press.

Raine, A. 1955. *Medieval York*. London: Murray.

Rodd, E. H. 1880. *The Birds of Cornwall and the Scilly Isles*. London: Trubner.

Ryder, M. L. 1961. Livestock remains from four medieval sites in Yorkshire. *Agricultural History Review* 9: 105-110.

Ryder, M. L. 1964. The history of sheep breeds in Britain. *Agricultural History Review* 12: 1-12; 65-82.

Ryder, M. L. 1970. The animal remains from Petergate, York, 1957-58. *Yorkshire Archaeological Journal* 42: 418-428.

Ryder, M. L. 1976. The origin and history of British breeds of sheep. *Ark* 3: 166-172.

Ryder, M. L. and Stephenson, S. K. 1968. *Wool Growth*. London: Academic Press.

Silver, I. A. 1969. The ageing of domestic animals. D. Brothwell and E. S. Higgs (eds.), *Science in Archaeology*. London: Thames & Hudson: 283-302.

Simmons, J. 1974. *Leicester Past and Present*. London: Eyre-Methuen.

Skeel, C. 1926. Cattle trade between Wales and England from 15-19th centuries. *Transactions of the Royal Historical Society* 4th Series, 9: 135-158.

Stanes, R. 1969. Devon agriculture in the mid-eighteenth century: the evidence of the Milles enquiries. M. A. Havinden and C. M. King (eds.), *The South-West and the Land*. Exeter Papers in Economic History: 2, 43-65.

Stephens, W. B. 1958. *Seventeenth Century Exeter: A Study of Industrial and Commercial Development 1625-1688*. Exeter: Exeter University Press.

Thirsk, J. 1967b. The farming regions of England. J. Thirsk (ed.), *The Agrarian History of England and Wales Volume IV 1500-1640*. Cambridge: Cambridge University Press.

Thirsk, J. 1967b. Farming techniques. J. Thirsk (ed.), *The Agrarian History of England and Wales Volume IV 1500-1640*. Cambridge: Cambridge University Press.

Thirsk, J. 1976. Seventeenth century agriculture and social change. P. S. Seaver (ed.), *Seventeenth Century England*. New York: New Viewpoints: 71-110.

Trow-Smith, R. 1957. *A History of British Livestock Husbandry to 1700*. London: Routledge & Kegan Paul.

Uerpmann, H. P. 1973. Animal bone finds and economic archaeology: a critical study of 'osteo-archaeological' method. *World Archaeology* 5: 307-322.

Veale, E. M. 1957. The rabbit in England. *Agricultural History Review* 5: 85-90.

Welldon Finn R. 1967. Devonshire. H. C. Darby and R. Welldon Finn (eds.), *The Domesday Geography of South-West England*. Cambridge: Cambridge University Press: 223-295.

Wheeler, A. 1969. *The Fishes of the British Isles and North West Europe*. London: Macmillan.

Wheeler, A. 1977. The fish bones. A. Carter and H. Clarke, *Kings Lynn Excavations*. Society for Medieval Archaeology Monograph Series 7.

Wheeler, A. and Jones, A. 1976. Fish remains. A. Rogerson, Excavations on Fullers Hill, Great Yarmouth. *East Anglian Archaeology* 2: 131-245.

White, K. D. 1970. *Roman Farming*. London: Thames and Hudson.

Wilkinson, M. R. forthcoming. The fish remains from Okehampton Castle (Report submitted to the Department of the Environment 1979).

Woodward, D. M. 1967. The Chester leather industry 1558-1625. *Transactions of the Historic Society of Lancashire and Cheshire* 119: 65-111.

Yealland, S. and Higgs, E. S. 1966. The economy. R. H. Hilton and P. A. Rahtz, Upton, Gloucestershire. *Transactions of the Bristol and Gloucestershire Archaeological Society* 85: 139-142.

Yellen, J. E. 1977. Cultural patterning in faunal remains: evidence from the !Kung Bushmen. D. Ingersoll, J. E. Yellen and W. MacDonald (eds.), *Experimental Archaeology*. New York: Columbia University Press: 271-331.

Youings, J. 1969. The economic history of Devon 1300-1700. F. Barlow (ed.), *Exeter and its Region*. Exeter: Exeter University Press: 164-174.

Youings, J. 1974. *Early Tudor Exeter: The Founders of the County of the City*. Exeter: Exeter University Press.

INDEX